The Picturesque And Historical Guide To ... Jersey

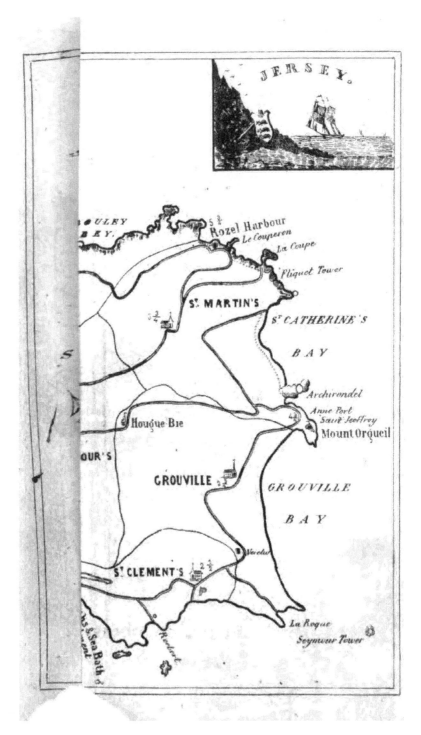

THE

PICTURESQUE AND HISTORICAL

GUIDE

TO THE ISLAND OF JERSEY:

COMPILED FROM THE BEST AUTHORITIES,

BY THE REV. EDWARD DURELL, A.M.,

AND

INTERSPERSED WITH LITHOGRAPHIC
DRAWINGS,

BY P. J. OULESS, ARTIST.

SECOND EDITION.

Jersey :

PUBLISHED BY PHILIP JOHN OULESS,

50, PARADISE ROW.

PAYNE, PRINTER,

AT LE FEUVRE'S, BOOKSELLER,

BERESFORD STREET.

PREFACE.

THE following little Work is in Three Parts, with head-ings to, the different Chapters for the facility of reference, a plan which it is hoped will be found advantageous.

The First part (*from Page* 1 *to* 72), is an abridged History of Jersey, compiled from the best historians, mixed with original matter, and continued to the present time. The want of a cheap and accessible edition of this kind had long been felt as a desideratum.

The Second Part (*from Page* 76 *to* 134), is mostly confined to a Description of the Town of St. Helier, and its contiguous maritime, and military establishments.— The author avails himself of this opportunity to acknow-ledge the valuable information he has received from his venerable friend, the learned M. De Gerville, the French antiquary of Valognes, on the ecclesiastical antiquities of this Island.

The Third Part (*from Page* 135 *to* 193) consists of a Tour, in Six Chapters, to the most interesting localities in Jersey. It is an original selection, rather than a compilation from OULESS' SCENIC BEAUTIES OF JERSEY, published a few years ago, the Explanations and Descrip-tions of which were written by the author of this Work, for which he now solicits the patronage of the Public.

A certain part of the materials had never appeared before ; the rest is a compilation, which, though it has been selected from the best authorities, can have no claims to originality. This always happens, when the novelty of the subject has already been long exhaustèd, by its previous appearance in numerous publications. It is therefore only by something new in the style, or by some particular arrangement of the matter, that an old subject can be placed in a more striking point of view, and have the merit of being made more interesting to the Reader.

After this candid acknowledgment it would be superfluous to crowd the following pages with marginal references to the numerous authorities, which it has been advisable to consult in the course of preparing this Publication.

The strictest impartiality has been observed throughout, so as to speak of men and things, as if every prejudice had been removed by the distance of some centuries from the actors in those busy scenes ; but at the same time to shrink from no statements, which can be estabished by facts, and to profess no opinions either inconsistent with the purest loyalty to our Sovereign, or at variance with the warmest attachment of Jerseymen to their native island, or to the well-being and the permanency of its local interests.

St. Helier's, Jersey,
   June, 1852.

TABLE OF CONTENTS.

INTRODUCTION.

HISTORICAL SKETCH OF JERSEY.

CHAPTER I.

CHAPTER II.

CHAPTER III.

CHAPTER IV.

CHAPTER V.

CHAPTER VI.

CHAPTER VII.

CHAPTER VIII.

CHAPTER IX.

CHAPTER X.

THE PICTORIAL GUIDE TO JERSEY.

PART II.

CHAPTER 1.

CHAPTER II.

THE PICTURESQUE GUIDE TO JERSEY, &c.

PART III.

CHAPTER I.

Introduction.—Sir Walter Raleigh's Government
of Jersey.—Dr. Hooper, and the Climate.—Its equa-

INTRODUCTION.

—

Situation of the Channel Islands, and of Jersey in particular.—Its proximity to the coast of France.—Its conformation and general appearance.—The fertility of its soil, and its abundant supply of fresh water.

IN a deep bay on the coast of Normandy, which takes its name from the far-famed monastic and chivalrous Abbey of Mount St. Michael, at an easy distance from the continent, lies a group of small but fertile Islands, which now form the only feeble, but interesting remnant of the ancient Duchy of Normandy, but which is now better known by the general name of the Channel Islands. These consist of Jersey, Guernsey, Alderney, and Sark, with some smaller ones of little importance. Of all these, Jersey is the largest, the most populous, and the nearest to the coast of France, it has also the most considerable proportion of fruitful and cultivated land. These islands are further highly favoured in point of situation and latitude, lying open on one side to the British Channel, and in one of the mildest portions of the temperate zone. St. Michael's Bay forms an extensive curve, which recedes to a considerable distance into the French coast, and sweeps on from Cap La Hague in Normandy, to Cape Fréhelle in Britany. The whole of that long range of coast is commanded in time of war by the naval forces of Great Britain, which are stationed at those islands.

Jersey lies the most southerly of this group, and as this little work is particularly intended to assist strangers in their excursions there, it will be unnecessary to say any thing further about its sister islands. We may therefore begin by observing, that Jersey is situated in 49 degrees of North latitude, and 2 degrees, 22 minutes, West longitude of London. Geographically speaking, it cannot be denied that it forms a very approximate appendage of the French continent, the nearest points of which, are not at

A

the distance of more than five or six leagues. These are the small fishing towns of Carteret and Portbail, from the latter of which the Jersey markets receive a plentiful supply of provisions. The sea in the intermediate channel is shallow, and as there is a tradition that Jersey, at some distant period, was, by some violent commotion or other, separated from the continent, if such an event did ever happen, it was probably at that place. It is at the eastern end of Jersey, where the sea leaves dry at low water a ridge of low rocks, of sand banks and of shingle, about three miles in length, which is well known by the local name of the " Bank du Violet," near the extremity of which, and on a higher rock, Seymour's Tower was built about sixty years ago. It was from that point that it was found, on actual soundings not many years back, that the water in the middle of the channel, is not more than 40 feet at low water, and about 80 feet at full tide. How frail then, yet how extraordinary a barrier is this, which has kept two nations distinct from each other in their manners, their laws, and their religion for almost a thousand years!

The other French ports in the neighbourhood of Jersey, are Granville, at the distance of 10 leagues, and those of St. Malo and Cherbourg, at the distance of about 12 leagues each ; the latter of which has of late years become a formidable naval establishment, which in case of any future war with France, would require to be watched by Great Britain with particular vigilance.

In reckoning the distances to the nearst British possessions, they are as follows :—

> To Guernsey, about seven leagues.
> To Alderney, about ten leagues.
> To Weymouth, about twenty-five leagues.
> To the Isle of Wight, about thirty leagues ; and
> To Southampton, about forty leagues.

The form of the Island is that of an irregular paralellogram, running from South-east to North-west. Its greatest length is about twelve miles, and the average breath may be estimated at full five miles, but in no part does it exceed seven miles. It has been ascertained by a recent survey, that its surface contains from 30,000 to 40,000 acres. From this total must of course be deducted some tracts of sandy downs and rocky coasts, with a few other waste lands only adapted to the growth of wood or furze.

The appearance of Jersey is that of an inclined plane towards the South. The same conformation is also observable with some exceptions of high and rugged tracts of coast on its western and eastern boundaries. Part of the eastern coast, commencing at Mount Orgueil, and the whole of the northern shore as far as l'Etac, in St. Ouen's parish, form, with but few interruptions, a range of cliffs rising abruptly from the sea to the height of from 200 to 300 feet. This natural defence renders the island in those places nearly inaccessible. The internal rocks are in general mere naked ridges, forming here and there promontories projecting into the sea, a circumstance which adds to the rapidity of the tides and currents, and varies their courses. In several places the rocks are loosely blended with other stony substances, or are in a state of great disintegration. Hence the violence of the tides has formed some deep inlets, and scooped out several caverns, where occasionally, in such confined situations, the water rises to the perpendicular height of 40 or 50 feet, whence the spray is dashed about in every possible direction. It is at a narrow interval from these rugged cliffs that the land begins to decline towards the southern coast, which in several places is nearly on a level with the sea. The slip of table land, which runs parallel between the northern and southern coasts, and from which the waters flow towards either, is on an average not above a mile wide. In this respect, Jersey displays a striking contrast with Guernsey, the southern boundary of which shoots up into high rocks from the water, and declines towards the north. It is principally owing to this difference of position, that there is such a marked variety in the nature of the soil, and in the temperature of the atmosphere in the two islands, which considering the small distance between them, would otherwise be inexplicable.

In general the strata of the rocks run from North to South, thus following the form of the island; but those layers are usually more inclined than the declination of the surface. No part of the island rises to an elevation of more than from two to three hundred feet, the highest localities of which are tracts of table land, gradually sloping towards the sea, particularly on the southern coast

Those elevated parts are at small distances from each
other, and intersected by deep, and in general by narrow
vales, which run from North to South. The sides of those
vales are bounded by steep and sometimes even craggy
declivities; but more frequently they are planted with
timber, or thickly set furze and brushwood. Those slopes
are generally too steep to be cultivated to advantage, and
are therefore left in their unproductive state. At the
highest elevation of those slopes begins the table land, to
which they seem to serve as embankments to prevent it
from falling into those vales. Under this point of view,
the country presents as it were an appearance of hills,
which had been truncated and compressed, to form the
irregular surface of that table land. These numerous
vales have copious rivulets of water, which run through
them, when they again receive the accession of an infinite
number of tributary streams, which flow into them from
a thousand springs. On which account their is not perhaps
any spot in the world which is more bountifully supplied
with fresh water. The comparatively long course of those
rivulets is particularly advantageous to so small an island
as it enables it to have a greater number of water-mills
than it would have been possible to erect under different
circumstances.

A thousand springs gush from th' adjacent hills,
    And pour their waters thro' embow'ring groves,
And grassy meads, in fertilising rills ;
    While as the eye along the landscape roves,
With rapid glance, a living picture moves,
    Of happiness in each secluded vale,
Where dwells a num'rous race, where labour proves,
    That frugal food and pleasure shall not fail,
While health is in the clime, and coolness in the gale.

Notes on Falle's History, p. 373.

HISTORICAL SKETCH OF JERSEY.

CHAPTER I.

Origin of the name of Jersey.—Its occupation by the Celts and the Druids.—The conquest and government of the Romans.—Its ancient connection with France.—Conversion of the Inhabitants.—Canonisation of Saints.—The Islanders become a distinct people.—Invasions of the Normans, and their ravages on the coasts of France.

A SHORT sketch of the historical recollections of the Island of Jersey may not be unacceptable, the more so as they become dim and uncertain, in proportion as they recede into the darkness of distant ages.

The name of Jersey itself is involved in obscurity. The most common opinion is, that it is of a Roman origin, and that its present Latin name of Cæsarea, is merely derived from the adjective of Cæsar, which has since been corrupted into Jersey. This subjection of Gaul to the Romans lasted for four centuries and a-half; and it is probable that during that long period, some of the Cæsars might have been attracted to this favoured spot; but it is very unlikely that a place then of so little importance, should have been visited by Julius Cæsar, who was the first Roman emperor, and the conqueror of Gaul, to whom the building of Mount Orgueil Castle is commonly attributed. Indeed, tradition seems to have been fond to assign exclusively to Julius, whatever has been done by any others of the Cæsars. The name of Cæsarea is however very ancient, from its being mentioned as an island of the British Ocean, in the Itinerary of the Emperor Antonius Pius, who reigned 150 years after Christ. It results from this that Jersey was already an island, and that if it had ever been severed from the continent, it must have been at a period of very remote antiquity.   It is however certain, from the remains of Roman entrenchments, from the occasional finding of medals, and from the vicinity of the island to the Roman colony at Coutances, that it had been occupied by that people ; but in the absence of positive proofs, conjecture and probability may be allowed, however imperfectly, to supply their place.   We, therefore, assume that the rule of that people continued, till they were themselves expelled from Gaul by the invasion of the northern barbarians.

As to the period which preceded the Roman conquest, little can be said about the state of the island.   Like the rest of the neighbouring countries it had been under the influence of the superstition of the Druids from the various cromlehs or religious memorials of those enthusiasts, which have been discovered here.   It was during their ascendancy, that the Castle of Mount Orgueil was first erected ; for the present buildings seem to be Norman. A post so impregnable then, was not likely to have been neglected.   The druidical worship, however, continued long after the establishment of the Romans, nor did it disappear from the land till the propagation of Christianity had prospered on the ruins of those odious rites.   It is therefore for those different reasons, I am inclined to believe, that the name of Jersey is not of a Roman, but of a Celtic origin ; and that it is derived from " Caer," a rock, and " ey," an island, from which a Roman would naturally write Cæsarea, though it would correspond better with the rocky cliffs, which line so large a part of its coasts.

It may be further mentioned in this place, that some of the earlier writers sometimes refer to Jersey under the name of Augia, as if it had already been so known under the dominion of the Celts, and before the coming of the Romans.   Whether they were correct in using that name, it is now impossible to ascertain, and indeed it would be superfluous to inquire.

The first period of the history of this island is that which existed under the administration of the Druids and the Celts, which ended in the conquest of Gaul by Julius Cæsar, a little before the Christian era.   The particulars of those times are so much involved in fables, that they may be continually disputed, or what is still more discouraging, that although some of the facts may be true, they are totally void of interest to the general reader.

The government of the Romans lasted till the subversion of their empire in Gaul. During those four centuries, Gaul became comparatively civilized. Roman colonies were founded and flourished, while the old superstitions of the country gradually disappeared with the propagation of Christianity. This, however, was the general effect of Roman administration at large, but it is impossible to say. how far those multiplied benefits extended to all the remoter provinces, or to the island of Jersey, which was then poor, unimportant, and with a scanty population. It has indeed preserved no vestige of the residence of the Romans, except some mouldering encampments, and a few solitary medals of some of the Emperors, which have occasionally been found. Even tradition is silent, whether the commanding fortress of Gorey, or Mount Orgueil, was ever a Roman station.

After those conquerors had been expelled from our shores, the Francs, a nation of barbarians, who had issued from the wilds of Germany became in their turn the conquerors of our soil and founded an empire, which has since been known as the French monarchy. That warlike nation breaking out of their native recesses, spread themselves like an inundation far and wide. Under the two first dynasties of the kings of France, their empire gradually increased, till it comprised all the countries, which are included between the Danube and the ocean. That immense tract was divided into eastern and western France, part of the latter of which constituted the country of Neustria, whose lower province, at a subsequent period, was ceded to the Normans, and assumed their name. The ancient Neustria was a maritime province, of which the Channel Islands had been considered as parcels, and consequently during those ages, they were integral dependencies of the great kingdom of France. The duchy of Normandy, which succeeded, was also a maritime tract, but much smaller than the ancient Neustria.

The period of that ancient French sovereignty extends over a duration of almost five hundred years, or from the foundation of that kingdom about the year 420 to the ces-

sion of the province of Neustria to the Normans in 912.
The transactions of those times are meagre and scanty, or
refer to men and actions, which have long ceased to be
interesting, and whose effects have no influence on the
present state of society. Those events were the wars,
and the degeneracy of the first dynasty of the French
sovereigns, the invasion of the Saracens, the wars and the
establishments of Charlemagne, and the subsequent declension, and final ruin of his family. These were indeed
great historical events, but their consequences have passed
away, till they have become in the present state of society
to be no more, than the shadows of an empty dream.
Moreover, every history of this kind belonging to the general efforts of a great country, cannot with propriety be
referred to, as being the local history of any particular
district. Therefore, the annals of the Channel Islands,
and of the neighbouring parts of the continent, may be
dispatched in a few words. In the first place, the various
elements of the population, whether Celtic, Roman, or
French, were melted into one general mass, from which
arose a new language and a new nation, which now constitutes the modern French. The amalgamation of the
usages of the ancient natives, of different countries with
the Romans, who conquered them, have in like manner
occasioned the origin of the several nations of modern
Europe, till every section of its large families, have become proud of their nationality, and by means of progressive improvements and variations, have still further
widened the lines of separation. This is more particularly
striking in the case of the Frenchman, the Spaniard, and
the Italian, who though originally sprung from the same
stock, have since spread themselves out into distinct nations. Hence, under this point of view the Channel Islands
were strictly French, and constituted a small part of that
monarchy during the first five hundred years of its existence, a long period indeed in the course of human generations, and more than sufficient to impress the indelible
traces of a national character. This will account for
many of the laws, and other local peculiarities of the
inhabitants of those islands, and why French has been
retained, notwithstanding their change of religion and of
political circumstances, as their vernacular language.

It is to this period of French connection, that we must refer the complete conversion of the natives to the Christian faith. It is well known that the Roman Empire was Christian at the time of its destruction, unless it might have been in some of its remote and yet half civilized provinces. When, therefore, one reads of the successful labours of the missionaries, who came from Wales into Armorica, since Britany, and into the neighbouring districts, it must be generally understood that, their exertions were directed to eradicate the remnants of the druidical, and of other pagan superstitions from the country, and to convert that part of the population, which consisted of the hordes of northern barbarians, who had settled in their conquests. Be that however as it may, it is evident that the general propagation of Christianity, the formation of dioceses, the building of churches, and the establishment of a regular priesthood are referable to this period.

Most of the churches in the Channel Islands have retained the names of their patron saints, whose career was either very obscure, or at most but locally known. Many of them had been the founders of their own churches, who after having spent holy and useful lives in the service of their respective congregations, were considered by them as being of a superior order, to whose tutelary guidances they might commit their worldly and spiritual concerns. It would seem as if every church then enjoyed the right of canonisation, and that it is to circumstance that we must attribute the great number of saints, whose origin is unknown, and whose names have never been canonised. It is not commonly known that the canonisation of saints is not to be found in the early ages of the church, and that the first instance of it in the Romish Church happened in the year 923, in the case of St. Uldric. At present that church does not canonise any one till a hundred years after the death.

Another effect of that early connection with France, is that it has left some indelible marks on the national character of the inhabitants, such as on their laws, their language, and their habits, which sufficiently prove that they are not of a British origin, but that they have been so much modified through a long series of changes and variations, that their protracted connection with the Normans, and subsequently with the English, has rendered them a distinct people, in every respect essentially different from the two powerful neighbours, who almost enclose their narrow limits on ever side.

The latter part of this period was productive of the most extraordinary events. The Normans, a northern nation as their name imports, and who seem to have been the same people as the Danes, who so long ravaged England, extended their piracies to the coasts of France, and rendered them the scenes of their havoc and desolation. Their incursions began under Louis I.; the son of Charlemagne, and lasted about eighty years, or to 912. The success of those invaders had the effect of increasing their numbers, and rendering their incursions more frequent, and more formidable. Their track was marked with the most frightful horrors, and with scenes of the bitterest distress. It belongs, however, to the history of France to expatiate upon those calamities, which are but incidentally mentioned in this place, so far as they affected the Channel Islands, and the adjoining continental province of Neustria. The weak successors of Charlemagne, were unable to resist effectually the violence of those invaders; but it was in the reign of his grandson, Charles the Bald, that matters grew infinitely worse, the whole of which was spent in endeavouring to oppose a barrier to their ravages. By means of their light vessels they ascended the rivers, and penetrated into the heart of the country, where they plundered, and burned the towns, and shed such torrents of human blood, that the ruin and devastation, which followed in their course, could hardly find a parallel in history. Those pagans were gross and brutal idolaters, and strongly addicted to all the superstitions of their god Odin. It was this which made them wreak their rage, particularly upon churches, monasteries, and religious persons ; and indeed everything that was Christian, was exposed to their wanton and unmitigated barbarity. There were no places in the neighbourhood more exposed to the predatory incursions of those barbarians than the Channel Islands, near which they necessarily had to pass as they ranged along the coasts of the Continent.

CHAPTER II.

As JERSEY had long before been converted to Christianity, it was there that the Pagan Normans left a signal instance of their ferocity. There lived then here a holy man, who had long been distinguished for the piety, and the austerity of his life. The name of that recluse was HELIER, whose little solitary cell, which he had chosen for his retreat from the world, is still to be seen on a rock near Elizabeth Castle, and still retains, after so many ages, its primitive name of the Hermitage.

They put this holy man to death under those aggravated circumstances of cruelty, which gained him the reputation of a martyr and a saint. The anniversary of his martyrdom, according to the ecclesiastical calendar of the Cathedral of Coutances, happens on the 17th of July. The island itself became famous in after times, on account of this undaunted, and devoted man ; and still more so, when after a long interval, a Norman nobleman, of the posterity of those who had murdered him there, founded an abbey on the spot, which had been hallowed by his martyrdom, and dedicated it to his memory, by calling it the Abbey of St. Helier. It was then, also, that on the neighbouring shore, and in the sight of the Hermitage, was laid the first foundation of the town of St. Helier, which has in the present age become a large, commercial, and important sea-port.

After the Normans, as above stated, had continued a predatory kind of warfare for about eighty years, the king of France, Charles the Simple, finding that all his efforts to repel those merciless invaders, were unavailing, sought to make a compromise with them, and by making a cession of some part of the kingdom, to save the rest. Rollo, who was afterwards so celebrated, was then the leader of the Normans. The Archbishop of Rouen was sent to him with the overtures of a treaty. The emphatical words of the prelate on that occasion, have been preserved by the contemporary historians. " Will you, mighty Chieftain," said he, " be at war with the French, as long as you live ?" " What will become of you should death surprise you ?" " Do you think that you are a God ?" " Are you not a mortal man ?" " Remember what you are, and will be, and by whom you must one day be judged." After this solemn exordium, he proposed the terms of an accommodation, by which part of Neustria, containing all the fine tract of country, which extends 200 miles in length along the British sea, with a corresponding breadth, should be ceded to Rollo, and his successors for ever, to hold by fealty and homage to the crown of France, under the title and dignity of Dukes. It was further proposed to Rollo, that if he should embrace Christianity, the King of France would bestow his daughter Gilla upon him in marriage, as a pledge of sincere amity, and of perpetual peace between the two nations. The proposals were accepted, and the treaty was ratified by an interview with the two princes. Rollo was baptized, and his authority and influence, induced his followers to follow his example.

Those events happened in 912, when the Channel Islands were thus irrevocably severed from the French monarchy. Many vestiges of that ancient connection have remained, and though they may have been weakened or diminished during a long succession of ages, enough has however continued to establish a distant approximation to French habits. The Normans soon coalesced with the general mass of natives into a powerful and independent nation, the rival of France, and the principal check to all its schemes of aggrandisement. It is therefore at this period, that the Channel Islands may be said to have begun their new and permanent era, which may be still divided into two periods, the former of which continued as long as continental Normandy existed, as a great and powerful state, till through the incapacity and misrule of King John, it was subjugated by France. It had been separated from it for about 300 years, half of which had

elapsed since William had by conquest ascended the English throne. The latter period of the Normans is from
1204 to the present day, when the great mass of their
duchy has been merged again in the French monarchy,
and with their national independence, they have also lost
their national character. Hence, it may be said, and that
too with the proud conviction of truth, that the only
remnant of that enterprising people cannot now be discovered anywhere, except in the Channel Islands. This
short account of the early history of those noted Islands
may not be unacceptable to the general reader of this
little work, and it may also correct the notions of a few
individuals, who might perhaps pretend, that the present
brave and loyal inhabitants, are but a race of half foreigners, and little more than the population of some conquered territory, recently incorporated into the empire. It
is a striking feature in the history of the Normans, that as
soon as they had obtained a territorial settlement, the
greater part of them immediately embraced Christianity,
and in time became the most zealous supporters of that
beneficent religion, by their munificence in the erection of
churches, and by the large endowments, which they bestowed on religious houses.

The Normans became a quiet and orderly people, go-
verned by good laws, many of which are still in force.
Though some of them might not be calculated for our
times, yet, as a whole, they were quite sufficient for the
exigences of the people, for whom they had been designed.
The feudal system which the Normans established, and
which extended in all its ramifications from the Duke to
the lowest vassal, was the best which could have been
introduced under actual circumstances. Among a people,
where the sovereign had not the means of keeping up a
regular army, he was thus enabled to provide himself with
a military force by the divisions, and sub-divisions, of his
territorial resources among his retainers, who in their turn
were bound by their tenures, to assist him in repelling
any hostile aggression. Such armies indeed had but little
discipline, and were but indifferently qualified for distant
expeditions, or for protracted campaigns ; but they were
the only ones which could be raised by sovereigns without
revenues, whose nobility contributed in war nothing beyond their personal service, and when the commonalty

was yet too poor, and too unimportant, to increase the strength of the state, and render it independent of the nobles by their productive industry, and their consequent ability to bear the heavy load of accumulated taxes.

. When Rollo was baptised he had assumed the name of Robert, in honor of his sponsor Robert, Count of Paris, and one of the principal lords of Charles the Simple. He is, however, generally known under that of Rollo, an appellation under which he had acquired his former celebrity, and which could not be changed or eclipsed, by the assumption of any Christian name.

Rollo was, indeed, the commander of the largest of the Norman invasions, the result of which was the cession of Neustria in 942. The beneficial consequences of it, however, were not immediate in the diocese of Coutances, in which our island was then situated ; for some of the Norman chiefs, who had settled in these parts, had continued to be pagans, and it was even many years after, that the country had still much to suffer from an incursion of Haigrol, one of the Kings of Denmark. The reader may not be sorry to have the following quotation from the pen of the learned M. le Canu, in his history of the Bishops of Coutances :—

" The country might have expected better days after the conversion of Rollo. His example could not fail to have been highly influential, and in fact it had been so ; but that was but slowly produced in our diocese of Coutances ; for it appears from the registers of the Cathedral, that for more than a hundred years afterwards, the bishops could not come there but clandestinely to discharge their functions. It is not improbable that it was in consequence of that hatred to Christianity, that Count Riout armed the inhabitants of the neighbouring districts of Cotentin, and marched them to Rouen in 931 to attack the Duke of Normandy. The Normans of the Cotentin, though of the same nation as Rollo, reluctantly received him for their lord, as they had been settled in the country before him, and were independent of him. He therefore either dared not, or was unable to compel them to become Christians at the same time as his other subjects. He was in consequence obliged, to prevent the extinction of the Church of Coutances, to call his bishop near his person, and to grant him a place of worship in which he might officiate. During the seven days that the prince kept the white garment after baptism he made splendid grants to several particular churches ; his largesses extended even to the Convent of Mount St. Michael ; but Coutances had nothing, because that church was not then in a situation to receive any of those munificent grants.

" Those proud infidels, however, bowed their necks in the end under the yoke of faith. It was truly wonderful how those men were converted with all the sincerity of their hearts. Soon were they seen to lend a helping hand to repair the misfortunes, which had either been caused by themselves, or by their ancestors. They rebuilt the churches, raised the monasteries from their ruins, recalled the monks and the priests, and enriched the churches and convents. Thus in less than a century every thing was not only restored to its former state, but was even improved.

" The country had indeed changed its masters ; but it had not changed its usages, and the Norman Lords who had replaced the French lords, followed exactly the same course. In their civil institutions, they strictly adhered to the laws of the feudal system ; and with respect to religion, they built churches near the castles, or else they erected chapels in their very castles, where the priests whom they appointed there, were provided for at their own expense. It was there that every thing in Normandy was moulded after the example of France.

" The etymology of the names of most of our country parishes, is referable to the tenth and eleven centuries. Neither before that period is it possible to trace out any property belonging to any particular church such as tythes, or any revenues appropriated to the repairs of the sacred buildings.

" Every one of those lords annexed a provision to the church which he had built either for himself, or for his vassals. When they granted lands in fee, they retained the quit-rents for themselves, and the tythes for their chapels. The parochial priest or the chaplain, had to apportion that endowment into three parts ; the first for the fabric of his church, or for its repairs and maintenance, the second for the relief of the poor, and the third for the supply of his own personal wants.

"We have said perhaps too little about ecclesiastical discipline. One example will suffice. Till the twelfth century, baptism, except in cases of necessity, was not administered except on Easter Eve and at Whitsuntide. The neophytes, or the newly baptised wore during eight days a white garment, and a veil on their heads, which was called the chrismal. This became afterwards the perquisite of the church, and was used by the clerks for providing themselves with surplices."

(Evêques de Coutances, p. 96.)

It is from that period of independence and prosperity that the Normans are to be considered as a distinct nation, and the rival of France, till subsequently by their great victory at Hastings, they laid the foundation of a mighty empire, which has continued to aggrandise itself even after their political existence on the continent had been extinguished, and all the recollections of their departed greatness were only to be traced in the page of history. The Channel Islands have alone remained as a broken, but interesting wreck of that warlike people, and have continued through the vicissitudes of so many ages, to be faithful to their sovereigns, and unconquered ; a possession long anterior to the conquest of Britain, and the most ancient of all the jewels which now adorn its crown.

The name of Rollo has descended to posterity, not only as that of a great warrior, but as that of a quiet and benevelent prince, at once the conqueror, and benefactor of his new country. Some of his institutions have survived, and are still flourishing after the lapse of a thousand years. One of them, the Clamour of HARO, has in some measure been invested with an air of romance, as if a charm had attached to the sacred name, and as if protection could issue from the ashes of that virtuous prince, to preserve the weak from injustice, and to avenge the wrongs of the oppresed. It was a kind of solemn protest from any one who thought himself aggrieved, which was made in this form of words "HARO! O MY PRINCE, AID ME, FOR I AM WRONGED." It had the immediate effect of stopping all proceedings, till the matter could be accurately examined by a judicial investigation. A remarkable instance of this happened about 170 years after, at the funeral of his descendant, William the Conqueror. That clamour is still the common

St Brelade's

mode of proceeding in Jersey, when either of the parties imagines that the other is encroaching on, or deteriorating his real property. The matter is afterwards argued before the Royal Court of this island, and if the appellant cannot substantiate the aggression, of which he had complained, he is fined, as a punishment for having causelessly invoked, and profaned the sacred name of Haro!

It is not to be imagined, that at this early period of Norman prosperity, these islands were of the value and importance, which they have since acquired. They had no trade or resources, and their population was yet scanty and dispersed. They had, however, the invaluable advantage of being incorporated with those Normans, an heroical people, with whose national character they were identified, and in all whose triumphs, they had had their adequate share. In the absence of more positive evidence, it is a strong presumption of their weakness and poverty, that when the adjoining continent was daily being covered with the most magnificent, and the most expensive ecclesiastical foundations, the islands remained in their former insignificance, and had no other places of worship than small and rude chapels, which had been built in different parts of the country. The division by parishes did not yet exist; and St. Brelade, the oldest parish church in Jersey, is not of a higher date than of the beginning of the twelfth century. Previous to this, the public worship was celebrated in a great number of small chapels spread over the surface of the island. All these have gradually disappeared, some of them not yet many years ago, so that the only one which yet accidentally remains in rather a perfect state, is that in St. Brelade's church-yard.

Another fact not often attended to, is that the dynasty of Rollo still exists, and that his lineal heirs are still on the English throne. Many royal houses have indeed reigned in England; but they have all derived their right through females, who represented in direct descent the Norman blood of their illustrious progenitors. The salic law is a mere accidental mode of conveying inheritance, and where that law has not been adopted, the female who inherits, continues the Royal race; for it would be ridiculous to pretend that such an interruption in the male line, did constitute a change of dynasty. Under that point of view, the family on the throne of England, is the first Royal House in Europe, and even more ancient than that of France, as on a reference to dates, it is evident tha t Rollo had already been acknowledged for a sovereign prince before Hugh Capet had become, by election, or rather by usurpation, the first king of the third race of the sovereigns of that country.

CHAPTER III.

Period of Norman Independence.—Consequences of the Battle of Hastings.—Dissensions in the family of William the Conqueror.—Deviations in the succession of the Crown.—Henry I., and his son, Prince William Regnault De Carteret.—Tancrede de Hauteville.—Abbey of St. Helier.—Matilda and the Abbey of the Vow.—Henry II., and his line of French Coast.—Continental Normandy re-conquered by France.—National character of the present Channel Islanders.

IT is not perhaps generally observed, that the period of Norman independence can be divided into two portions of almost equal duration. The former of these begin with the dismemberment of Neustria from the crown of France in 912, and comes down to the battle of Hastings. It forms the first and most important epoch in the history of independent Normandy. It was then that the national character was fully developed; and that what they wanted in numbers and in resources, they compensated in energy and perseverance.

The latter is that from the battle of Hastings to the conquest of Normandy by the King of France, and its final incorporation with that monarchy. The connection with England made that latter country the principal seat of power, and it had evidently a tendency to impair the nationality of the Normans, and to prepare them by degrees to acquiesce with less reluctance to submit to sink again into a French Province.

A period of 154 years elapsed from the establishment of Rollo to that of the battle of Hastings, which placed William on the throne of England. That battle was indeed one of the most important that ever happened in the history of mankind, and whose consequences have been, and are still felt, after almost 800 years, not only in the frequent struggles between Great Britain and France, but in the system of European politics in general.

During that period seven dukes reigned in Normandy, who were all distinguished princes, who successfully maintained their independence and aggrandised their dominions.

A new era began for the Normans, and for the islands in particular, who thus became firmly united to England, from which they have never since been separated. Nothing has been recorded of these islands during the reign of the Conqueror, in which they were exclusively concerned. But though all memorials of the fact are lost, it is but a fair presumption to suppose, that many of the vassals from the island followed their sovereign in his expedition against the Anglo-Saxons, and shared with him, more or less, in all the dangers and advantages of the conquest.

William, as it is well known, was particularly unfortunate in his family, and perhaps there is no example in the whole range of history, of brothers more ambitious, more unprincipled, or more unnatural, than the sons of William. The most valuable part of the patrimony of Robert, the eldest son, was usurped by his brother, William Rufus. Robert, a brave and warlike prince, entered largely into all the visionary schemes of the crusades. He repaired to the Holy Land, where after performing prodigies of valour, and materially contributing with his Normans to the success of the first Crusade, he might have been elected King of Jerusalem, had he not been particularly desirous of returning to his own country. But misfortunes followed him on his return, and he was a second time prevented from succeeding to the English throne. His brother Henry had taken advantage of his absence, and had usurped his crown. It was in vain that Robert endeavoured to recover his birthright ; for having been disappointed, his brother Henry stripped him of his remaining duchy of Normandy, made himself master of his person, and doomed him to a perpetual imprisonment in an obscure castle in Wales, where he lingered till his death for twenty eight years. It is said, that to disable him from ever appearing again in the world, he had caused him to be deprived of sight. Such aggravated instances of the misfortunes of the great, are seldom to be found, even in the annals of the blackest times, and cannot be read without the mingled feelings of horror and of sympathy.

A question would here arise, whether the reduction of

Normandy, and the captivity of Robert by Henry I. could be considered as a conquest of the latter province by England ; and that in consequence the Channel Islands, with the rest of the duchy, became a conquered dominion annexed to that kingdom.   But the idea of conquest implies an aggrandisement made at the expense of an independent state.   But this could not be considered to be the case in the dissensions of the sons of William the Conqueror, which was a civil war, or rather a rebellion against the lawful heir ; for such undoubtedly it would have been esteemed, had he prevailed.   It could not also have been a conquest, as Henry I. only brought over to him, either by force or by intrigue, all the dominions which had been held by his father.   It is indeed impossible at this distance of time, to examine with accuracy the reasons which had led to those unnatural dissensions : but it is evident that according to the strict and unvarying rules of right, Henry I. was an usurper of his brothers dominions, and that to palliate his wrongs, his flatterers might have subsequently set up a claim for him, which rested on conquest.   But no ingenuity or adulation can ever hallow crime, or throw a veil over the imprescriptible rights of justice.

It is a peculiar feature in the history of England, that although its sovereigns since the conquest have all descended from the same dynasty, there have been frequent deviations from the regular line of succession, when princes of the royal blood, have stepped into the enjoyment of the rights of some elder branch.   This happened in the case of Henry I., who usurped the right of his elder brother ; and a modification of the same principle occurs in the Act of Settlement, which set aside the claims of the House of Stuart to the crown.

Henry I. was now at the height of all his glory, being nearly the most powerful monarch of his time, and left without a competitor to dispute his usurpations.   But the vengeance of Heaven, however slow it may be, is certain, and the evil days which awaited the descendants of the Conqueror were not yet exhausted.   Prince William, his only son and heir, perished by shipwreck, near Barfleur in Normandy, on his return to England.   In that young Prince the male line of the Conqueror became extinct ; and Henry himself, who had never recovered from his loss, died a few years after :—a signal instance of the just retributions of Providence, and of the perfect vanity of unprincipled ambition.

The reigns of Stephen, Henry II., and Richard I., were atteded with many events, which though not of a political nature, naturally affected the islands. Some of them were the following :—

The celebrated Castle of Gouray, or Mount Orgueil, whatever might have been the date of its original foundation, its actual fortifications were decidedly Norman ; though, as we have said before, it is not probable that a post, in those ages so apparently impregnable, should have been left unfortified by any of the ancient possessors of the island.

The first crusade where Duke Robert distinguished himself, introduces the noble name of De Carteret, which acquired afterwards so much merited celebrity in the local history of Jersey. Regnault De Carteret, who followed that chivalrous prince in his expedition to the Holy Land, had large possessions in Jersey, as well at the small town of Carteret, on the adjoining continent. Hence it is highly probable that several of the natives of Jersey went in the train of their feudal lords in that religious but chimerical enterprise.

It had not been many years before this, that Tancred, a Norman gentleman of Hauteville le Guichard, a village near Coutances, left Normandy with his twelve sons in search of adventures, in the course of which, having conquered the southern parts of Italy, and the island of Sicily, they founded there, what is now called the kingdom of the two Sicilies. The family of those chivalrous champions maintained themselves on that throne for about 150 years, or till 1195.

In 1125, William, the son of Hamon, founded the Abbey of St. Helier, at the place where that holy man had suffered martyrdom from the Norman pagans 250 years before. It was built on the present site of Elizabeth Castle, and was liberally endowed with revenues in the island, and on the Continent. It flourished for a period of sixty-two years, when it was annexed to the Abbey of the Vow at Cherbourg on the following occasion. The Empress Matilda, the mother of Henry II., having, during a voyage from England, encountered a violent storm, and being in danger of perishing, she vowed that if it should please God to pre-

serve her, she would build an Abbey, and sing a hymn of
thanksgiving to the Holy Virgin, on the first land that she
might reach. Soon after this the coast of Cherbourg appeared, when the pilot, in the exultation of the moment
addressed her these words—" Sing, O Queen, here is the
land." The name of " Chanterine" has remained to the
creek, in which she landed at Cherbourg, where she sang
her hymn, and built the Chapel of St. Mary of the Vow.
That chapel, though often destroyed, was as often rebuilt,
and is still used, as a place for holy worship.

Matilda soon after founded an Abbey, which from its
site, and the accomplishment of her vow, was named the
Abbey of Cherbourg of the Vow. Many years afterwards,
in 1185, Walter, the then archbishop of Rouen, and his
brother Benjamin, then Abbot of Cherbourg, obtained a
papal bull, and the king's permission to annex the Abbey
of St. Helier in Jersey to the former, though the latter
was the more considerable of the two. Robert, the Abbot of St. Helier, was preferred to Cherbourg ; but that
annexation was highly prejudicial to the Abbey of St. Helier, which became in consequence a priory dependent on
Cherbourg, and was not allowed to have more than a prior
and five canons. The connection between those two religious houses continued till the Reformation. But mark
the instability of human affairs ! The very ruins of the
Abbey of St. Helier have disappeared, and nothing but
the small and solitary hermitage of its martyred patron
now remains. The Abbey of the Vow has also been dismantled in the storms of the French revolution. It was
there that Louis XVI. lodged, when he visited Cherbourg
in 1786. Who could have then thought that so soon it
would be as the ruined Marius sitting on the ruins of Car-
thage ? The venerable Abbey is now used for a naval hospital, and of all its ancient buildings, nothing remains but
the hall and the refectory.

Henry II. was the most powerful of all the Norman
princes ; but it does not seem that any of the English historians have remarked that his continental dominions included all the coast of France, from the frontiers of Spain
to the utmost limits of Normandy ; his subsequent acquisition of Britany by the marriage of one of his sons with
the heiress of that duchy being within that line. Perhaps
that was thought to be of little consequence in that remote

age, or that the possession of such a large extent of coast, with several sea-ports, would in future times secure to France a large naval preponderance. Could it have then been taken advantage of, as it would be now, the superior fortune of Henry, would have stifled the growth of the French monarchy, which was yet in its infancy. But how transitory is human greatness! In less than twenty years from Harry's death, that mighty colossus of power had fallen to the ground, never to rise again.

We are now come to the inglorious and disastrous reign of John, which dismembered for ever continental Normandy from Britain. The distinct character of that pious, high minded, and warlike people is to be sought for in the days of its prosperity and independence, from Rollo to the reign of John. After that eventful period, the Normans became as aliens in the land of their fathers, their national pride and spirit left them, a few great families emigrated, the rest submitted;—but the islands alone remained unsubdued. It was thus that the great mass of the people lost their nationality, by adopting French manners and customs; while the gentry vied in subservience and adulation to their new sovereigns, who after three hundred years had thus dispossessed the weakest and the most criminal of the descendants of Rollo. As a people, the Normans were now politically extinct, except in these diminutive fragments of them, which from that time began to form a separate community in the Channel Islands, which in their usages, their appearance, their laws, and their language, still shewed a spirit of independence, and that aversion to a French connection, which proved that they differed as much from that people, as they do from any other foreign European nation.

The Jerseymen of the present age are the descendants of these vassals, who followed William the Conqueror to Hastings; of those knights who, with Duke Robert, expelled the infidels from the Holy Land, or of those chivalrous adventurers who accompanied Tancred to found a new kingdom in the south of Italy.

The present race of Islanders has not degenerated; though the enterprises of desolating warfare, and the individual exploits of romantic bravery, have been exchanged under better auspices for the more beneficial extension of commerce and navigation. Nor have they been less

renowned than their ancestors for having produced the
loyal, the brave, and the wise in such men as Sir George
De Carteret, Lord De Saumarez, the late Duke of Bouillion,
and the two Brocks. A country that can produce such
men, may be proud of its nationality, and cannot but be
eminently solicitous to continue in its distinct and separate
state. So far then from being a conquered or dependent
dominion, they may vie in nationality, with the Anglo-
Saxon, or with any other people of Europe. That nation
has now lasted for more than nine centuries, with a distinct
language, and with a distinct permanence of jurisdiction,
which has been guaranteed to them, by a long succession
of sovereigns, as the reward of their inviolable and undiminished loyalty. And may that attachment to their
British connection be for ever ?

CHAPTER IV.

Effects of the Conquest of Normandy.—Character of King John.—The Islands escape subjugation.—The Norman proprietors lose their lands in Jersey.—Loyalty of the De Carterets.—Constitutions of King John.—Charters repeatedly granted by other Kings.—The Islands as neutral ports.—Frequent French Invasions.—Repulse of Du Guesclin from Gouray.—The reigns of Richard II., Henry II., and Henry IV., uninteresting.

A NEW ERA began for the Channel Islands with the beginning of the thirteenth century. We are now come to that highly important period, when Normandy lost its national independence, and was again reduced to the form of a French province. That dismemberment was felt by England as a severe humiliation, and occasioned the most bitter national animosities, which caused almost interminable wars for almost 300 years; nor did the chimerical projects of recovering the English continental provinces, seem to have been abandoned till the accession of the house of Tudor in 1485. It is not here our object to examine whether the loss of those territories, which were at a distance from the centre of the monarchy, and which could hardly have been defended from the attacks of a powerful and inimical nation, was not ultimately beneficial to Britain. But as to the islands, it was fortunate for them that they were not swallowed up in that general dismemberment; as that circumstance had the effect of strengthening their connection with England, and brought them at once within its more immediate protection, but without strictly incorporating them with Britain. That dismemberment gradually assimilated them to British views and feelings, and in course of time put them in possession of all the blessings that belong to British subjects, such as civil liberty, industry, wealth, and the protestant religion.

The character of King John belongs to history, and after so many ages, it may be judged without the influence of fear or the prejudices of partiality. It would be unneces-

sary to enter into minute particulars, when it is well known,
that it was the most unfortunate, and the most degraded
reign in all the annals of Britain.   After having been an
undutiful son, and a faithless brother, he usurped the crown
over the children of a deceased elder brother.   The son,
Prince Arthur, disappeared, and it is supposed was murdered, by the orders or the connivance of his unnatural
uncle; and his sister, the Princess Eleanor, of Britany,
was doomed to a perpetual imprisonment in the Castle of
Bristol, where she lingered for forty years till her death.
Had such horrors existed in private life, what state of
society would have tolerated such a monster?   Such an
offender would not have been suffered to exist; and history
shows that tyrants, in almost every case, have not escaped
the punishment which was due to their crimes. The King
of France, who was the suzerain lord of John, took
advantage of the indignation and the disaffection which
those atrocities excited among his subjects.   John was
three times cited to appear before the High Court of Parliament of the King of France, in his quality of Duke of
Normandy, to answer to a charge of felony for the murder
of his nephew.   To such an indignity, and its consequent
danger he refused to submit, and the summons having
been three times repeated, judgment was awarded against
him for contumacy and parricide, in consequence of which
his extensive dominions in France were ordered to be
seized and reunited to that crown, as having been forfeited
by his condemnation.

Philip Augustus, the King of France, was appointed to
carry the sentence into execution,—a commission which
he gladly accepted, and to which his crooked policy had
long been directed.   The sentence considered as an act of
that severe justice, to which the high as well as the low
ought to be amenable, had been deservedly incurred, and
if it had only reached the guilty sovereign personally, he
would have fallen unpitied.   But on the other hand, there
can be no doubt that nothing can justify the defection of
the subject to a foreign enemy, when such conduct would
be productive of the greater evil of revolutionising a country, or subjecting it to a foreign yoke.

Philip was highly desirous of reducing Normandy, which,
ever since it had been separated from France, had given
more trouble and uneasiness to that country than all its

neighbours put together. He therefore, lost no time to direct all his efforts to succeed in that enterprise; and here it cannot fail to be remarked, from the example of John, how weak and how wretched was that prince, who lost his best means of defence in the alienation of the love of his people. The Normans had not yet degenerated from their ancient valour. No nation had ever been better trained to the use of arms, when on account of their vicinity to the French territory, they and their ancestors had been kept in an almost continual state of warfare. They hated them as being their old and natural enemies, with whom they had had so many encounters during the whole of the long period—they had been settled on the continent as a separate nation. The spirit of disaffection was now, however, widely spread, and they suffered themselves to be an easy conquest to Philip. Some of the towns made a moderate resistance; but it was Rouen that stood out the longest. The greater part, however, opened their gates voluntarily to Philip, and received him within their walls as a deliverer. A change so sudden and so unexpected in the minds of men could have been occasioned by hatred of the usurpation of their King, and of his cruel treatment of the orphans of his departed brother. It would, however, have been wiser for the Normans to have resisted, and trusted that the reign of John would soon pass away, when a more virtuous sovereign would bring back things into their ancient channel, rather than have submitted to a foreign power, to prevent a temporary usurpation, which would break down their ancient independence, and weigh them down under the galling yoke of the severest oppression. Thus happened the separation of Normandy from England, 137 years after the two countries had been united under one sovereign, by the decisive victory of Hastings, by William the Conqueror, and it became again a province of France, 312 years after it had been erected into an independent state.

It has always been thought extraordinary that the Channel Islands were not subjugated with the rest of John's dominions. It was not because they could have offered no effectual resistance, or because their sovereign could not have given them any assistance. Nor was in that age the naval superiority of England sufficiently established to have prevented an invasion. It is true that the islands

were twice invaded during that reign, and that the invaders were as often repulsed by the bravery of the inhabitants, whose loyalty in the general defection of Normandy
had been unshaken for their hereditary sovereign.   It is
not, however, to be supposed that if King Philip had made
any serious attack upon the islands, he would not have
succeeded, considering their then defenceless state, from
the scantiness of their resources, and the poverty of their
population.   Scarcely any memorials of those invasions
of the islands have remained; and if they were at all
seized by the enemy, it is equally evident that they were
not permanently occupied.   All this may be granted without any disparagement to the honour or the loyalty of the
inhabitants.   Probably the islands owed their safety to
their being of difficult access, and to their being thought
of litle value.   Philip had too many objects of greater
importance on which to fix his attention, and could not
spare a sufficient force to succeed in an enterprise, which
would have repaid neither for the dangers, nor for the expenses to be incurred.   Be that however as it may, the
islands were preserved; and their isolation from Normandy linked them but the closer to their sovereign, and
rendered them if possible still more desirous than ever of
the continuance of their British connection.

As the result of this separation was that the Channel
Islands would have in future to rely for protection on
either of the two great neighbouring countries, they wisely
made their election of Britain, from which have been derived so many beneficial consequences, which have been
handed down unimpaired to the present generation.   As
they became English, they gradually acquired advantages, which they would have never gained as French; or
rather they have been exempted from all the misfortunes
which would have attended their connection with France,
—such as that of a long depression under a despotic government, which would have left them in their original
poverty and insignificance, and made them the victims of
religious thraldom and intolerant superstition.   But above
all, they have been enabled to escape from the terrible
and sweeping vortex of the French revolution.

Several of the Norman proprietors had also lands in
Jersey, which they lost by confiscation for having submitted to the Conqueror, and preferred to stay in the

country, where they had their most valuable estates. But among the few, who had the courage to adhere to their sovereign, one noble family made the sacrifice of their patrimony in France, and settled on the lands which they still possessed in Jersey. That family was the De Carterets, the descendants of that Regnault De Carteret, who went with Duke Robert to the first crusade. And, indeed, for high deeds of glory and for local celebrity, through an uninterrupted continuation of ages, their name might compete with some of the most distinguished in the empire. It is, perhaps, a pleasing reflection to have sprung from a race of worthies, but that is of little value, if their descendants are in their declension, and rely on a long ancestry, which seems, in fact, but to upbraid them with their own inferiority. But, be that as it may, that family had the peculiar felicity of preventing, under King John, the islands from being seized by France, during the troubles of that prince, by repelling two distinct invasions within a few years. Again at a later period they delivered Jersey from the usurpation of the Count De Maulevrier; and at another time already ancient, but not so remote, Sir George De Carteret adhered with inviolable fidelity to the two Charles's in their adversity,— nor yielded Elizabeth Castle to the enemy, till after a protracted siege, and after having been the last to surrender in all the British dominions. A rare example of merit and good fortune, and almost unexampled in any history, that the same family should have saved their country from foreign conquest twice ; and again to have been "once," the last, whom dire necessity compelled to surrender their country to the galling yoke of a regicidal usurpation.

King John visited the islands about the end of his reign ; and is said to have been particularly careful in repairing its strong holds, and placing its various harbours and landing places in the best state of defence. Gorey Castle, or in a most recent time, Mont Orgueil Castle, was already a considerable fortress, which after the repairs and the improvements laid out at differentItimes, was till the invention of artillery deemed to be impregnable.

That King, who, under the intimidation of his English barons, has yielded to them the great Charter, granted during his stay in Jersey, another Charter to its loyal inhabitants. As the former had been extorted by violence and compulsion, so this was the effect of approbation and gratitude on the part of the sovereign. That charter has, in fact, been for the islanders what the great character has been for the English. The Constitution of King John, as that charter is called in Jersey, have proved of the highest importance to its liberties, as being the foundation of all the rights, privileges, and immunities, which it enjoys to this day ; the principal of which is, that it should be free from all foreign dependence, and own no objection to any other power, or be under any other restriction than the immediate control of the crown, as administered by the Sovereign in Council. Hence the inhabitants are amenable but before a court in their own island, where they are to be judged by their own laws, and by native judges, whom on the authority of the charter, the freeholders themselves elect. The charter calls them *sworn* coroners, or jurats ; and, indeed, the popular election of coroners in England may probably be of the same origin, and be a remnant of the same usage. The constitution of Jersey was decidedly of a Norman origin, the enjoyment of which was confirmed to the inhabitants of that charter. It has affixed the seal to their nationality, which has enabled them to retain their language, manners and customs ; and by preventing them from being totally assimilated to the English, it has continued them, as it has been already said, to be the only feeble, but interesting remnant of the once celebrated Norman nation.

From this period all connection of the islands with Normandy ceased, which began to be considered both in war and peace, as a foreign country, and an integral part of France, with all those feelings of aversion and hostility, which till very lately had for so many ages existed between the two great countries. Henceforth the history of the islands becomes so much linked with that of England, that it is to be sought in that of the latter country.

A few general features have however distinguished the islands during that period. Through so many reigns, and under so many sovereigns of very different characters and pursuits, their loyalty to them has been zealous, sincere, and persevering ; while their attachment to England has ever been, under all circumstances, unbroken, and undiminished. Another feature in the history of the islands is, that they have been the favoured subjects of the Kings

of England ; and that their charter, originally granted to
them by King John, has been ratified, confirmed, and
enlarged by most, if not all, their sovereigns till James II.
On account of their exposed situation and liability to
invasion, they obtained the most valuable privileges and
immunities ; the most important of which is, that they
are allowed to enjoy in every part of the empire all the
rights of Englishmen, by being put on the same footing as
natives, and not as aliens. For a long time also the islands were by mutual consent considered as neutral ports,
where the vessels of the belligerents had a free access to
come to, and go from, without any hindrance or molestation for the purposes of trade.   They were well situated
for the grant of such a neutrality ; and as they were small
and poor, such a singular privilege did not then excite
those naval or commercial jealousies, which made its continuance incompatible with a more advanced state of
society.   That principle still existed under Henry VIII. ;
but how much longer it remaiued is unknown.

It is nevertheless remarkable that this neutrality was
merely commercial, and did not extend beyond the facilities it gave for trading to the islands ; for duriug the
whole time that it continued, the rage of hostility between
England and France remained unmitigated, and the islands themselves had to repel some of the most critical
invasions of their limited territories.

The third feature of the annals of those islands, is the
frequent invasions to which they have been exposed, and
the perpetual state of alarm and anxiety, in which they
have ever been kept in time of war.   Those invasions
were, however, particularly freqnent during the reigns of
the Plantagenets ; though it may be surmised, that many
of them were merely predatory incursions, which indeed
inflicted severe injuries at the time, but which led to no
permanent results.   It is likewise very extraordinary,
that the islands were not alternately taken and retaken, as
might have been expected ; but that in every instauce the
enemy were repulsed. It is, hower, an exception, that
Guernsey was occupied by the Fiench during three years
in the early part of the reigu of Edward III. or 1338.   It
was granted by Philip de Valois to his son John, afterwards King of France, the same who was taken prisoner
at Poitiers by Edward the Black Prince.

After passing over several of the invasions of the islands, under the successors of John, which, probably,
were not very important, and of which scarcely any memorials remain, till the reign of Edward III., about 1331,
when the French sent a powerful fleet to cruise in the
British Channel. Southampton was taken and pillaged;
and it was then that the island of Guernsey fell into the
hands of the enemy. Jersey escaped from conquest by
the obstinate resistance and loyalty of the inhabitants,
whose invaders were at length compelled to raise the siege
of the then impregnable fortress of Gorey Castle. Its
Governor, Drogo de Barentin, one of the principal gentlemen of the island, fell in one of the attacks upon it. The
name, though disguised, was probably the same, as that
of the noble family of the Barringtons in England, and
had a common origin from the small town of Barenton in
Normandy. The name of that noble family might have
had also some reference to Barentin, a village near Rouen,
through which the new railroad to Paris passes. He was
succeeded in his command by Renaud De Carteret, a native of the island, and not inferior to the brave du Barentin in valour and capacity. The defence was continued
by the chivalrous Renaud, till the seige was raised.

Part of the reign of Edward III., was a series of vic-
tories and triumphs, and during that period the islands
were in no danger. The peace of Bretigny between the
two crowns secured the connection of the islands with
their natural Sovereign, the King of England. But unhappily the successes of Edward were not of long continuance, and his old age was chequered by the most fatal
vicissitudes. The military affairs of France were directed
by the Constable de Guesclin, when hostilities were re-
newed some years after the peace of Bretigny. The
Constable was one of the ablest, and the most successful
generals of his time, who soon recovered nearly all that
Edward had acquired on the Continent during the late
wars.

The island of Jersey had then to sustain the most formidable invasion, which it had yet experienced. Du
Guesclin, after having taken several towns in Britany,
among which was that of Brest sailed from that port to
invade Jersey with an army of 10,000 men. He was accompanied by the Duke of Bourbon, and some of the

chivalry of France. The whole of this invasion is fully
described in the history of Britany by D'Argentré. It does
not appear that the inhabitants attempted to oppose his
landing. On the contrary, they left the enemy masters of
the open country, and placed under God all their hopes of
deliverance in the strength of their castle, and in the
courage of the brave men, who had been entrusted with
its defence. Nothing was omitted on the part of the assailants, after the manner of carrying on sieges in that age.
Some of the outer walls were thrown down by sap, but that
did not affect the main body of the place. The castle was
several times attempted to be carried by storm, but every
time it ended in the disaster and repulse of the assailants,
some of whose bravest men perished in those attempts. But
though the besiegers could not take the castle, neither did
this resistance oblige them to raise the siege. On the other
hand, the besieged found famine to be growing among
them, with all the despondence which arises from a protracted and hopeless resistance. At length both parties
being wearied out with this kind of warfare, they came to
a composition, by which it was stipulated that the be-
seiged should surrender the castle, unless they should be
succoured before Michaelmas day ; that in the mean time
there should be a suspension of hostilities, and that the
Constable after having received hostages for the performance of the articles, should break up his camp and depart. Such compositions were then frequent, the terms
of which were generally executed with good faith. The
practice seems indeed to have been introduced to save the
honor of both parties, when they were equally tired with
the length of the siege. The Constable in consequence
returned to Britany, where he was soon after informed,
that an English fleet was out at sea, with the professed
object of relieving the castle. This seasonable relief prevented the composition from being carried into effect, and
the castle remained untaken. Thus ended that invasion,
as one might say, most gloriously for Jersey ; since its
fortress had been perhaps the only one which had baffled
all the efforts of that great and fortunate warrior, when
every other place which had belonged to England on the
Continent, and which he had attacked, had invariably
fallen in the struggle.

The two succeeding reigns of Richard II. and Henry

IV., produced no events worthy to be mentioned, except a predatory invasion of Jersey during the latter reign, which was easily repulsed.   Henry V., having been informed of the great exploits, which had been performed in the defence of Gouray Castle, changed its name to that of Mount Orgueil, which it has retained ever since.   He was succeeded by Henry VI., a weak and inoffensive, but misguided and unhappy prince.   The latter part of his reign was particularly unfortunate, on account of the disputed claims to the crown by the rival houses of York and Lancaster. Though it does not appear, that the islands took any active part in those civil wars, which desolated England at that period, the consequences of them, however, hurried on Jersey to the very verge of destruction.

CHAPTER V.

Reign of Henry VI.—Isle of Wight and the Channel Islands erected into a kingdom in favor of the Earl of Warwick.—Some account of the ancient Sovereignty of the Isle of Wight. Grants to the Fitz Osbornes, the Rivers, the Vernons, and the Beauchamps.—Sir Richard Worsley's account of that petty kingdom.—Conjectures and reflections on what would have resulted from an independence of the Channel Islands.

THE reign of Henry VI. was particularly unfortunate for the Channel Islands—not, however, on account of any part which they had taken in the contest between the rival houses of York and Lancaster—but because events occurred which had twice nearly separated them from their British connection, the former of which was when Henry Beauchamp, Earl of Warwick, was crowned King of the Isle of Wight and of the Isles of Jersey and Guernsey, in 1445, by Henry VI., and afterwards created Duke of Warwick by the same sovereign towards the latter end of his reign.

It is known from history that the Isle of Wight had been anciently held as an independent sovereignty. William Fitz Osborne was one of the principal Norman warriors who had followed William the Conqueror, and fought with him at Hastings. He was made Earl of Hereford; and in 1070, that monarch bestowed upon him the Isle of Wight, to be held by him as freely as the King himself held the realm of England. This Fitz Osborne was William's kinsman and confidential friend, and had been marshal of the Norman army at Hastings. This Lord held his high dignity but a short time, having fallen in battle four years after on the continent. He was succeeded by his second son Roger de Bretteville, who having been afterwards concerned in a conspiracy to depose the King, he lost the Isle of Wight, and his earldom of Hereford reverted to the crown. As to himself he was condemned

B

to perpetual imprisonment, in which he ended his days in 1086.

The island was again granted to a subject by Henry I., in 1105, who gave it to Richard de Rivers, Earl of Devon, from whom it descended to his son Baldwin. That baron having espoused the cause of the Empress Maud, endeavoured, but in vain, to defend this territory against King Stephen. He was obliged to fly for his life; but afterwards, when an accommodation took place, between the contending parties, he was restored to his possessions. After having passed lineally through several of the Rivers, the Isle of Wight devolved by marriage, in 1184, to William de Vernon, a collateral branch of that family, whose descendants held it till 1293, when Isabel de Fortibus, the heiress of the last Earl, surrendered her interest in that island to King Edward the First, who annexed it to the crown from which it has never been again separated except during two short interruptions. The former happened in the case of Henry Beauchamp, who was crowned King of the Isles of Wight, Jersey and Guernsey, in 1445; and in that of Richard Widvil, the father-in-law of Edward IV., who was created Lord of the Isle of Wight, in 1466. The reason that he did not also obtain the sovereignty of the Channel Islands was, that Jersey had not yet been rescued from the power of the Count de Maulevrier.

This information about that Earl of Warwick who was King of the Isle of Wight, is derived from Leland, Dr. Heylin, and Sir Richard Worsley's History of that island, whose work contains an engraving of "Henry Duke of Warwick, King of the Isle of Wight," and his sister, who married the Duke of Somerset. They are represented kneeling before an altar. Sir Richard gives also in a note, a Latin extract from Leland, from which it appears that Henry, Earl of Warwick, enjoyed the high favour of Henry VI., by whom he was crowned King of the Isle of Wight. That monarch granted him also the Castle of Bristol, and the Islands of Jersey and Guernsey. Sir Richard observes, however, that very little notice has been taken of this singular event by historians. Selden has mentioned it in his titles of honor.

All these give a scanty information, indeed, with respect to the Channel Islands, although it proves that Warwick was in some sense a King: but of the extent of his royal jurisdiction, no precise information remains, nor whether he was to hold his sovereignty, as a fief, under the English monarchs. If so, it was certainly with more privileges than Barons had in general, and it would seem clear that all the revenues of those Islands were left at their disposal.

Worsley continues the account of what became of that petty kingdom, after the death of the Duke of Warwick. " In the 26th year of Henry VI., Edmund, Duke of Somerset, married the sister and heiress of Henry, Duke of Warwick, before mentioned, as King of the island ; who having some time before supplanted the Duke of York, in the regency of France, obtained a grant of this island, to him, and the heirs male of his body, in satisfaction, as it was alleged, for certain sums of money, due to him from the King's Exchequer, and for the duties of Petty Customs in the port of London, which were part of his inheritance.''

The Duke's prosperity was, however, of short duration, he died in 1455 ; and his two immediate successors, Dukes of Somerset, were involved in the misfortunes of the House of Lancaster, and both perished on the scaffold in 1463, and in 1471.

After that date this ephemerous kingdom vanished, and the islands of which it was composed have been inalienably reunited to the British monarchy. But it is never - theless a matter of curious speculation to inquire what would have been the probable consequences, if that limited territory had been suffered to exist as an independent state till our times ; and whether it might not have had a prospect of rivalling the histories of Geneva, of the Hanseatic towns, or of the republics of Lucca, or of San Marino.

In the first place, the importance of the Isle of Wight is too great and its vicinity too striking, for England to have consented to its permanent dismemberment. As to the Channel Islands had they been made into a small independent state, and their political existence had been suffered to continue, some very curious consequences might have been the result of such a measure. The feelings of the inhabitants would not have been violated, by having been transferred against their will to a foreigner, as in the case of Maulevrier ; but as their new sovereign, the Earl of Warwick, was a gallant soldier, a man of high rank, and an Englishman, their

subjection to him would have been received with far less
reluctance ; still an insuperable objection would have remained, that it would have dissolved their English connection for ever.

Had their independence been suffered to remain through
the forbearance, or the mutual jealousies of the foreign
powers, their situation would always have been precarious,
like that of other small European states, some of which
after so many revolutions are still suffered to exist.   But
they would have gained nothing by that political change ;
for with the right to govern themselves without any external controul, they would have incurred all the evils of
civil discord, such as distracted the modern Italian republics during the middle ages.   In point of trade, they
would have had all the advantages of free ports, and their
position might have rendered them as prosperous as any
of the Hanseatic towns of Germany.   Nevertheless, in
another point of view, their insular situation would have
been unfavourable, as leaving them more exposed to attack,
and more likely, from their continual intercourse with
strangers, to be brought into collision with foreign powers.
Malta was the last of the smaller European islands, which
had maintained its independence, but it expired in 1798.
As to Corfu and its dependencies it has since been
formed into the Republic of the seven Ionian Islands,
which was the consequence of the downfall of the once
powerful republic of Venice.   Its existence is rather nominal than otherwise, for even that empty shadow of
national independence, could not be maintained without
the vigilant interference, and the incessant protection of
Great Britain.

But is it more conducive to the happiness of a small
community to be possessed of political independence,
rather than to form part of a large one ? The small republic is seldom involved in the quarrels of its distant
neighbours, but it has fewer securities against domestic
commotions, occasioned either by a tyrannical aristocracy,
or by the licentiousness of an ungovernable mob, and
above all, by the perpetual danger of being swallowed up
to suit the convenience, or the aggrandisement of some
more powerful state, a striking instance of which has
occurred within a short time by the annexation of the
Republic of Cracow to the Austrian Empire.

A large government is better enabled to protect all its subjects, and to overawe the efforts of hostile, or evil disposed neighbours ; but on the other hand, the different parts are often brought in contact with interests to which they are foreign, and the parts are generally sacrificed to promote the power of the whole mass ; or if the government is despotic, every thing is rendered subservient to the pride, the caprices, or the ambition of one man.

CHAPTER VI.

Queen Margaret of Anjou.—Her intrigues to deliver Jersey to France.—Mount Orgueil Castle surrendered to the Count de Maulevrier.—His endeavours to render his government popular.—Philip De Carteret, of St. Ouen, and six of the parishes resist him for six years.— Fall of the House of Lancaster.—Arrival of Sir Richard Harliston at Jersey.—Mount Orgueil invested by sea and land.—The French garrison capitulates.—Charter and acknowledgment of Edward IV.—Perrotine Famget.— Misfortunes of Harliston.—Policy of Henry VII.— French invasion under Edward VI.

MARGARET OF ANJOU, the Queen of Henry VI., was of the Royal blood of France, a woman of uncommon talents, and of a most persevering spirit. In proportion as the fortunes of her husband declined, she sought for new resources to retrieve his losses. She accordingly negotiated with Peter de Brésé, a French nobleman, and Count of Maulevrier, to put him in possession of the Channel Islands, as the consideration for espousing her cause. The negotiation, however, was carried on apparently without the knowledge of the King of France, who was apprehensive that it might have involved him in a war with England. Maulevrier was a leader of some military reputation, and found no difficulty in raising a body of 2,000 veterans, who were desirous to try their fortunes with him in an expedition to England. A part of that body was landed in Northumberland where between the swords of the enemy, and the storms which they encountered at sea, the greater number of them perished.

Maulevrier had now to receive his reward, and the Queen gave orders that he should be put in possession of Mount Orgueil Castle. Sir John Nanfan was then governor of the Castle; he farmed the island under the crown, and it is even uncertain whether he was a British subject.* To throw, however, as dark a veil as possible over that nefarious transaction, and to save appearances for the governor, it was contrived that he should be surprised and seized in his bed. As all resistance in that case became impossible, he immediately surrendered the island. Thus for the first time did treachery introduce an enemy within the gates of Mount Orgueil Castle. As soon as the Count de Maulevrier received intelligence of his success, he repaired to Jersey, to establish his newly acquired authority. No acclamations of the people welcomed him to its shores. It was everywhere the reluctant submission of a high spirited and loyal race, and that sullen, but expressive silence, which dared not openly to mourn over the loss of their independence. The Count, however, had recourse to all the means of insinuation which might gain him popularity, and allay feelings of a discontented population. He assumed the title of Lord of the Isles, under his Sovereign Lord, the King of France, and at a solemn assembly which he held in Mount Orgueil Castle, he confirmed all the privileges of the inhabitants in as full a manner as they had ever enjoyed them under any of their former Kings. He also made some valuable additions to their charter, defined the manner of administering justice, and ordered a register to be kept of the transfer of all property, an improvement which was not however carried into effect till almost 150 years after, under the government of Sir Walter Raleigh. When aversion or hatred have once taken root in the human mind, it is seldom that either gentle usage or forbearance can exchange them for loyalty and affection. The Count was coldly received by the assembly; and out of the Castle, he was openly resisted. The island is divided into twelve parishes; the six eastern of which, as being nearest to the Castle, reluctantly submitted to the usurper. The other half made an obstinate resistance, and repelled all the efforts of Maulevrier during six years. This was probably

* The name is written " Nanfan," in all the old manuscripts, which a careless transcriber would easily corrupt into " L'Enfant," especially as there would be a kind of connection between the name, and the negligence of that officer. His case affords a striking resemblance to that of Major Moses Corbet's surrender of Jersey, on the 6th of January, 1781.

no more than a war of skirmishes, as the Count and the inhabitants were severally left to their own individual resources ; for the contest would soon have been decided, if the Kings of England or France had taken an active part in those hostilities. It was then that Providence raised a distinguished patriot to avenge the wrongs of the islanders, in the person of Philip De Carteret, of St. Ouen, a name that seemed as destined in the annals of Jersey, to appear at the head of their countrymen on all great emergencies, to defend them and to succeed. After encountering many dangers, and performing individually some of the most chivalrous exploits, he checked the further progress of Maulevrier, during those six eventful years, till at length the hour of deliverance arrived. Had such a man, and with such inadequate means, rescued his native island from thraldom in the heroical ages of Greece, his name would have descended to us as one of the brightest ornaments of the classic page.

After such a protracted state of hostilities, it was evident that neither of those chieftains could expel the other from the island ; but matters were now altered in England by the quiet settlement of Edward IV. on the throne. The Lancastrian party had been conquered, its chiefs had either perished in the field, or on the scaffold, while the few who had escaped from proscription lived in exile and poverty in foreign lands. It was not therefore likely, that Edward would ratify any compromise made by the Queen of Henry VI., to alienate any part of his dominions. He, therefore, fitted out a fleet to recover what had been lost, and gave the command to Sir Richard de Harliston, an officer of great merit and acknowledged loyalty. He first sailed down the Channel to the relief of Jersey, and having landed, he had an interview with Philip De Carteret, at his seat, with whom he concerted measures to reconquer the island. Their plans had been so well contrived that the enemy were surprised, and that one morning at daybreak they found the castle was invested by sea and land. The blockading fleet was indeed English ; but the land army which besieged the Castle being entirely composed of natives, under the command of the gallant De Carteret. The French commander to whom the defence of Mount Orgueil had been entrusted, did not show less courage and resolution. The fortress was not indeed attempted to be taken

by storm, as had been done in the siege, which it had sustained against the Constable Du Guesclin about one hundred years before; still there were many severe attacks,
in which many of the inhabitants were slain; and among
the rest, the "Seigneur" of Rozel, a gentleman of good
property, and one of their principal leaders.   The sallies
of the besieged were frequent, in attempting to break
through the lines of the besiegers; but they were fruitless,
and many of them paid for their temerity with the loss of
their lives.   The besiegers now limited their operations to
a blockade, and trusted for their eventual success to the
slow effects of disease and famine in compelling their
enemies to surrender.   This state of things lasted for nine-
teen weeks, during which time the besieged did all that
could be done by brave and skilful men to obtain relief;
but force and stratagem were equally ineffectual.   Their
friends on the continent, who from the short distance were
almost eye witnesses of the daily occurrences of the siege,
and who could not have been ignorant of the critical situation of the Castle, either dared not, or could not come to
their assistance.   At length Surdeval, the governor, and
Maulevrier's son-in-law finding the situation untenable, was
obliged to capitulate, which enabled him with his garrison
to return to France.

Never had Jersey been in so much danger before, and
never had Providence more signally wrought than it had
then for its deliverance.   The islanders gained much
honor by this siege ; and as the Castle had not yielded
but to famine, its former reputation of being impregnable,
still remained unimpaired.   Edward IV. granted them a
new Charter, with a special acknowledgment of their
good service, which clause has been inserted in every
subsequent Charter, to perpetuate the memory of their
exploit.   Those several Charters are on the whole but
repetitions of each other, as they were confirmed by each
sovereign at his succession, except on any particular occasion like the above, in which the retaking of Mount Orgueil was introduced.   Something of the kind is also
found in the Charter of Charles II., where a compliment
is paid to the loyalty of the inhabitants, who had thus
rendered themselves worthy of the Royal favour.

Perrotine Famget was the widow of Philip Johan, of
Guernsey, who had rendered services to Harliston during

the siege. According to Mr. Falle, the historian, that brave leader rewarded her with a liberal grant of money and ground rents ; which, according to the present value of money, might be estimated at about £300. This fact is mentioned as highly honourable to the several individuals concerned, and as a strong proof of the good feeling which then existed between the sister islands.

Harliston was rewarded with the government of the Channel Islands, and his daughter, an only child, was married to the eldest son of Philip De Carteret. Her marriage was one of extraordinary fecundity, and the high conjugal virtues which she displayed in adversity, have thrown over her an air of romance, and rendered her name one of the most distinguished of her sex. But after long years of prosperity, mark the vicissitudes and the nothingness of all human affairs! Harliston, in his old age, was attainted by Henry VII. for his attachment to the House of York. He fled, and died abroad in exile and poverty, a miserable dependent at the Court of the Dowager Duchess of Burgundy, a sister of Edward IV. Maulevrier, had, however, long before preceded him to an honourable grave, having been killed at the battle of Mont l'Hery in the service of Louis XI.

It is from the reign of Henry VII. that we may date the abandonment of the long cherished, but chimerical, project entertained by the Sovereigns of England to conquer France, or even to recover those continental provinces, which had once belonged to their ancestors. Hence wars between the two countries became either less frequent, or of short duration, and caused not those immense exertions, which exhausted the national resources. This state of things may be said to have lasted till 1688, and William III, when the restless ambition of Louis XIV., and a regard for her civil and religious liberties, revived the long dormant animosities of England to France. It must not, however, be supposed that during that long period of more than 200 years, the islands were not kept in an almost perpetual state of alarm. The short wars that occasionally happened, and even the very prospect of hostilities, were sufficient to produce that effect. Once only was the island in any real danger, when under Edward VI., a French fleet landed a considerable force at Bouley Bay ; but being attacked by the inhabitants, who were posted on the higher grounds, they drove back the assailants to their ships with great slaughter. Several hundreds of the enemy perished on that occasion. Hence, if Jersey had fallen in that unexpected attack, as Calais did a few years afterwards, it is probable that the enemy would have kept it, or at least would not have restored it but with reluctance, and under the influence of intimidation.

CHAPTER VII.

The Reformation and Annexation of the Island to the Diocese of Winchester.—Calvinism in Jersey.—Consequences of the Reformation.—Erection of Elizabeth Castle. —Sir Philip and Sir George De Carteret.—Charles II. visits Jersey twice.—Distinguished emigrants.—Charles I. and Hurst Castle.—The Commonwealth send an expedition against Jersey.—Sir George De Carteret opposes its landing without effect.—Siege of Elizabeth Castle.— It capitulates.—Oppression of Jersey till the Restoration in 1660.

HITHERTO we have considered the islands but in their political relations and importance, and their inhabitants as a brave and loyal race, the interesting remnants of a once mighty nation, who, by a singular good fortune, have, during so many ages, never been subjected to any foreign power; but have preserved their allegiance inviolate to the same and uninterrupted line of sovereigns, all lineally descended from each other for almost a thousand years. Our ancestors in common with the rest of Europe, had been labouring under the spiritual bondage of gross ignorance and degrading superstition. The hour was now arrived, when those grievous fetters were to be broken, and man was again to appear in all the dignity of knowledge and of truth. The Reformation spread early to the Channel Islands, and it would seem from a variety of records still remaining, that its doctrines had already taken a deep root there before the death of Henry VIII. Those doctrines afterwards rapidly increased among the inhabitants, and after having in some measure partaken in the religious oscillations and persecutions in England, the islands became decidedly protestant. In 1565, Queen Elizabeth finally removed them from the diocese of Coutances, and annexed them to that of Winchester. The annexation was not, however, immediately carried into effect; for the first reformers in the islands were protestant ministers from France, who

had fled from persecution in their own country, and who
imported with them, a leaning towards the opinions of
Calvin. Nor was this surprising, when it is considered
that the universal prevalence of the French language at
that time, would have offered an almost insuperable obstacle to any exertions of the English reforming clergy.
Hence, through the connivance of three successive governors, the islands, though strictly protestant, remained
unconnected with the Church of England, and formed for
themselves with their ministers a body of church discipline
on the model of that of Geneva. This is what has given
rise to the opinion, that the islands were originally cal-
vinistic. The state of things continued during the whole
reign of Queen Elizabeth, and a great part of that of James
I.; till after a certain degree of reluctance, and even
opposition, and it being known, that it was at the special
desire of the reigning monarch, they were indissolubly
united in doctrine and in practice to the Church of England.
This happened in 1623.

We are not, however, here to consider the beneficial
effects of the Reformation merely in a religious point of
view, but in their consequences, which added a still more
violent hatred to the heridinary aversion to any connection
with France; and rendered all the obstacles fourfold,
which would militate against any future incorporation of
the islands with that monarchy. As to ourselves, who are
persuaded that all their past and present prosperity has
been derived from their British connection, we cannot be
too thankful to Providence for that long and complicated
concatenation of events, which has been traced in this
historical sketch; and which has been productive of so
desirable an end, as the establishment of the civil and
religious establishment of this small but interesting portion
of the British empire.

Things, which in a general point of view would be
wholly uninteresting, assume a particular importance in
reference to some local object, with which they may be
connected. The great changes which had occurred in the
art of war, had destroyed the illusions which had so long
attached to the impregnability of Mount Orgueil Castle.
It was now found to be totally inadequate to the defence
of the island, and that in addition to the neglect of its fortifications, and the ravages of time, it was commanded by

a hill which rendered it untenable. Accordingly, Queen Elizabeth, in 1586, ordered another Castle to be built on a small island in St. Aubin's bay, on the site of the ruined Abbey of St. Helier. This is what is now called Elizabeth Castle, which, with Fort Regent, on the Town-hill, commands the Town and Harbour of St Helier. As for Mount Orgueil, it gradually decayed, as this new rival rose into importance ; and at this moment it presents little more than a mass of walls and buildings in the different stages of dilapidation, unable indeed to resist an invader, but still imposing to the beholder by its majestic site, and by the recollection of the chivalrous prowess of its defenders, who in the olden time so nobly repulsed Du Guesclin and Maulevrier.

The reign of Charles I. was productive of great misfortunes to the islands, for having inviolably persisted in their loyalty to their unhappy sovereign. Before the civil wars broke out, the celebrated Prynne had been confined for some time as a state prisoner in Mount Orgueil Castle, from which he was afterwards liberated. In 1643, the Parliament endeavoured by its emissaries to make itself master of Jersey ; but the loyal spirit of the inhabitants was too strong to be perverted by the intrigues of a few domestic traitors, and it soon declared for the King. Sir Philip De Carteret, of St. Ouen, and his nephew, Sir George De Carteret, appeared at the head of their countrymen on that glorious occasion. The former died soon after ; but the latter held the island for the king during eight years, in spite of all the efforts which could be made by the different factions, who had usurped the government of England. During those eight years Sir George, who was also an able naval officer, established, as it were, a small independent state, and made himself truly formidable to the Parliamentarian party, by the immense losses which his numerous privateers caused to their merchants, and by the constant relief and protection which he afforded to the several distinguished fugitives from England, whom their loyalty had exposed to danger and persecution. The Prince of Wales, afterwards Charles II., finding his situation untenable in the West of England, sailed from the Scilly Islands with a large retinue to Jersey, and remained there for some months till he retired into France. The island was then full of illustrious emigrants, the names of many of whom have been preserved in its local chronicles, and in the traditions which have descended to us of those times. The names of a few may suffice,—Sir Edward Hyde, afterwards the illustrious Chancellor, Lord Clarendon, the poet Cowley, and Sir Richard Fanshawe, the Prince's Secretary ; but who is now better known as the first English translator of the Lusiad of Camoens. As to Sir Edward Hyde, he resided above two years in Elizabeth Castle, where it is supposed that he wrote then a great part of his history of the Rebellion.

During the time that Charles I. was confined in Hurst Castle, near the Needles, and within the Southampton water, it is said that a plan was formed in Jersey to deliver the monarch from captivity by having surprised the Castle. Such a plan indeed would have been dangerous and difficult, but not altogether hopeless or impracticable. Sir George was of a daring and enterprising spirit, he had sufficient naval means in his power, and such was the ardent loyalty of many of his followers, that he would have found numbers eager to enlist in so difficult and chivalrous an enterprize. The scheme seemed to be perfectly feasible. As all vessels going to Southampton must pass near that Castle, it was imagined that four or five vessels from the island, disguised as traders, to prevent suspicion, might have a sufficient number of men concealed under the hatches, who on approaching the Castle, and on a given signal, would suddenly start forth from their lurking place, and scale the walls. This tradition rests on the authority of Mr. Falle, the respectable historian of Jersey, who mentions that he had often heard it mentioned not long after the Restoration and when he was still very young. It would not have been the first time that very strong fortresses had been taken by surprise, and their prisoners liberated. Had the attempt been made, and succeeded, the consequences which would have resulted from it, would have been immense,—the monarch would have been saved from the terrible catastrophe which awaited him, and his deliverers would have been rewarded with eternal glory. A dark and inexplicable fatality seems to have impended over the unfortunate Charles, which rendered ineffectual every effort that his friends ever made, or even intended to make in his favour.

After the death of Charles I., his son was proclaimed

here, it being then one of the very few places in all his
dominions where such a ceremony would have been practicable. In 1650, Charles II., with his brother James,
came over to Jersey, and resided for some months in Elizabeth Castle, from whence he went to France, having
been prevailed upon to embark in that rash enterprize to
Scotland, which ended so fatally for him and his adhe-
rents at the battle of Worcester. We pass over the de-
tailed accounts of those times, as they belong rather to
the history of England, than to a small local narrative
like the present, from which every thing that is not strictly
indispensable ought to be excluded.

The incessant clamours of the English merchants about
the losses, which they experienced from Sir George De
Carteret, drew on him at length the serious attention of the
Commonwealth. It was not only expedient to subjugate
those islands on account of the mischiefs, which they had
so often inflicted, but to punish them severely for their
presumption. It was, therefore, determined to invade
them, and a large fleet and army were prepared for that
purpose, and the command of the former was given to no
less a person than the celebrated Admiral Blake. The
troops on board amounted to 5,000 men, the command of
whom was entrusted to Haines, one of Cromwell's generals. After sailing from Portsmouth with a fair wind, part
of the invading fleet came in sight of the island on the 20th
of October, 1651, and on the same day came to anchor
in St. Ouen's Bay. Sir George had long foreseen that
invasion, and now he did all that a brave and prudent man
could have recourse to on such an emergency. He immediately collected his small body of regular troops, and
marched out with them and the insular militia to St.
Ouen's Bay, and resolved to make the best defence in his
power,—not that indeed with such inadequate forces he
could reasonably expect to succeed; but because there
is something in the generous mind, which forbids it to
despond, and because it is nobler to make an ineffectual
struggle in a glorious cause, than to yield tamely to an
enemy. Some of his followers had long been disheartened,
and were now wavering at the repeated ill-success of the
Royal cause, and into them he endeavoured to infuse the
same alacrity, which he possessed. On his reaching the
beach of St. Ouen's Bay, he took immediate measures to

oppose the enemy at their landing, and for three days he baffled all their efforts, during which time his little band was harassed with incessant watchings and fatigue in following the motions of the hostile fleet, as it hovered along the coast, and made demonstrations for landing.   At length, on the third night when the Royalists were exhausted with their severe and tantalising service, Blake succeeded in landing one of his battalions. They were immediately discovered, and Sir George charged them at the head of his little troop of horse ; the charge was desperate and bloody, in which many of the enemy were either killed or wounded.   As this nightly landing of the enemy had been unexpected, a great part of Sir George's infantry had dispersed the evening before to seek for provisions in the neighbouring villages, and could not therefore be collected again in time to support their gallant leader.   If then the infantry could have come up, it might indeed have protracted the contest ; but it was not to be imagined that Sir George would have eventually succeeded against such an overwhelming force.   In the mean time other troops were landed so fast, that all further opposition became useless, and that Sir George had no alternative left, but that of leaving the field, before his very inadequate force had been either overwhelmed and destroyed, or its retreat intercepted.   Sir George reached Elizabeth Castle in safety, in which he shut up himself, with a garrison of 340 men, among whom were several of his friends and some of the principal inhabitants of the island.   The open country was now abandoned to the invaders, who plundered the inhabitants, and made every part of it a scene of terror and desolation.   The strong holds which had formerly baffled so many foreign enemies, such as Mount Orgueil Castle, and the Tower, or Fort of St. Aubin, scarcely made any resistance.   Sir George was then summoned to surrender Elizabeth Castle, to which he indignantly returned a becoming answer.   The place was then regularly invested and besieged for several weeks, during which time it was cannonaded with 36-pounders from a battery on the hill, which now forms the site of Fort Regent, and unfortunately with some effect, as one of the shells fell into the old Church of the Abbey of St. Helier, under which were the stores for keeping the provisions, as well as the powder magazine. That shell broke through two strong vaults, and blowing up, it scattered around ruin and destruction ; but what was still more lamentable, it killed forty of the best soldiers in the garrison, besides armourers, carpenters, and other artificers, who are indispensably necessary in a siege. Notwithstanding this terrible blow, and a certain degree of consternation which spread through the garrison, Sir George by his prudence kept all quiet for the present, and held out some time longer till he could communicate with the king, who after the battle of Worcester had lately reached Paris in safety. Charles saw the hopelessness of Sir George's situation, and left him to act according to his own discretion. All hopes of relief being now at an end, and as no possible object could be answered by any further resistance, in addition that provisions were getting short, and that the garrison was daily becoming weaker by disease, and the ordinary casualties of war, it became imperatively necessary to treat for a surrender. Sir George obtained a highly favourable capitulation, after having sustained a siege, which, according to tradition, lasted six weeks and two days ; nor could it have been either much longer or shorter, as the Parliamentarians landed on the 22d of October, 1651, and took possession of that fortress on the 15th of December following. The surrender of Elizabeth Castle completed the conquest of the Island, which now for the first time was obliged to submit to the coercion of lawless force. It was, however, some kind of consolation, that the island remained as much as ever unsubdued by a foreign foe. It had now fallen, indeed, but it had been in an overwhelming struggle against the usurpations of revolted subjects.

' Evil years of oppression now rolled over the Norman Islands, which were treated with the greatest severity by Cromwell's military rulers. It was then that the parliamentarian individuals, who had excited so many disturbances in 1643, returned to the island, after an exile of eight years, and were restored to their estates, which Sir George had confiscated on his assumption of the local government. Michael Lemprière was confirmed in his office of chief magistrate, and held it till 1660, while D. Assigny was also rewarded with the living of St. Martin's, then supposed to be the best in Jersey, and enjoyed it, till he was deprived soon after the Restoration. At that auspicious period the Islands recovered all their ancient privileges, and obtained all the praises and other remunerations, which they had so nobly merited by an heroic and un-wavering loyalty of nearly twenty years, and in the worst of times.

CHAPTER VIII.

*Character of Charles II. in Jersey.—Revolution of 1688.—
Rising commercial importance of Jersey till 1779.—The
Prince of Nassau's attempted invasion.—Baron du Rulle-
cour's invasion in 1781.*

ANOTHER era in the history of the Norman Islands is, that
which commences at the Restoration, and extends to the
invasion of Jersey by the Baron de Rullecour, his defeat,
and the fall of the brave and ever to be lamented Major
Pierson.

Many traditions of Charles II. have remained in Jersey,
which cannot indeed be a matter of surprise, when we
consider the affectionate loyalty of the inhabitants towards
him, or the Royal favours which he conferred upon them.
The faults and the vices, which have cast so deep a stain
on the personal character of that monarch, were unknown
to our ancestors; nor indeed did they become prominent,
till they had been investigated by the impartial researches
of posterity, and become a part of the history of England.

Notwithstanding. their hereditary loyalty, they were
aware of the invaluable blessings of religious and civil
liberty, and cheerfully supported the principles of the Revolution of 1688, which placed William III. on the throne.
It was at that period that Mr. Falle, the patriotic historian
of Jersey, first distinguished himself as the Deputy of the
insular States to the British Government.

The commercial importance of the Channel Islands had
already begun to be understood. Charles II. had granted
the islanders a small duty on spirits for building a harbour
at St. Helier, till through subsequent additions it has
grown up to what it is at this moment, and enabled the
inhabitants to make such a considerable progress in industry, and in the full developement of all their local resources.

The annoyance which the islands occasioned to France
in time of war, had at length drawn upon them the particular attention, and the resentments of that formidable
power. The ambition of Louis XIV., and his interference

in favour of the House of Stuart, had long before revived
all the ancient animosities of Britain towards that country.
Hence when it became a part of her policy to spare no
expense in placing the Norman Islands in a proper state
of defence, it was, seconded, as of old, by the enthusiastic
zeal, and the voluntary privations and sacrifices of the
inhabitants.   From the operation of those causes, the
islands have been rendered almost inexpugnable, or at
least, they could not be attacked with any rational prospect
of success, but by a large naval and military expedition.
The difficulties under which this places France, contributes
also to their security ; because that power, would in
ordinary cases prefer to employ her resources, on objects
of more immediate importance, rather than expose herself
to disappointment and defeat in the attempt to make an
acquisition, the result of which would be so extremely
uncertain.

The period that elapsed from the Revolution to 1779,
was spent during peace in rapid internal improvements,
and in a state of great and perpetual alarms, whenever a
war broke out with France.   No actual attack, however,
took place ; the inhabitants grew rich, and though their
danger was imminent, it made them, if possible, but the
more attached to their country, like those nations, who live
contented in the land of their fathers, though incessantly
menaced by the convulsions of nature from the heavings of
the earthquake, and the eruptions of the volcano.

A French fleet came to an anchor in St. Ouen's Bay,
May 1st, 1779, and made a demonstration to land ; but
soon sailed off, without having accomplished that object,
or caused any mischief.   The reason of their sudden de-
parture has never been known ; but it is most probable,
that when they found the island could not be carried by
surprise, and that it would have required a much larger
fleet to succeed, they abandoned their project as impracticable, and retired from the coast.   The enemy did not
however lay aside their schemes of attacking Jersey, and
in less than two years, it was followed by the expedition of
the Baron de Rullecour.   This was the last time, and
perhaps the most critical that the natives of Jersey have
had to defend their homes ? and hence the name of Pierson
seems destined to live among them in the grateful recollection of every succeeding generation.   The best account

of that invasion was published a few years ago in the
"Scenic Beauties of Jersey," a collection of lithographic
prints, by MR. PHILIP JOHN OULESS, a native artist, and
is from the pen of the learned editor of the last edition of
Falle's History of Jersey, the REV. EDWARD DURELL, a
native clergyman, and Rector of the parish of St. Saviour.

CHAPTER IX.

WE had omitted to mention in the last Chapter, that after the Revocation of the Edict of Nantes, in 1680, that the islands offered a welcome asylum to the great number of French Protestants, who fled from the religious persecutions exercised against them in their own country. They were a peaceable and industrious race, and having been well received in Jersey, they prospered, so that their descendants have been so totally assimilated to ourselves, that they cannot any longer be distinguished from the general mass of the population.

The internal effect of the connection with England may be contained in a very short description ;—a large naval and military establishment, and fortifications, made, altered, pulled down, and then rebuilt, either at the times required, or rather as the views of the different Lieutenant Governors, either disapproved of, or recommended, as they were led by their desire of novelty, and of being distinguished each from his predecessor. From these, however, we may except the administration of the late General, Sir George Don, from 1806 to 1814, who was the first to introduce the construction of good roads in Jersey.

It has been also a feature of recent times, that the inhabitants have ever been most anxious for the preservation of their immunities and privileges, and have always shown themselves particularly zealous of anything, which might be construed into an encroachment or an abridgement of them by the British government.

The events of 1781, were followed by the peace of 1783, and a renewal of friendly and commercial relations with France. During that interval of peace, Field Marshal Conway, the Governor, and the Duke of Richmond, then at the head of the Board of Ordnance, visited the island, and many improvements were adopted in consequence of their suggestions. In 1785, a large Druidical Temple was found on the Town Hill, which now forms the site of Fort Regent that monument was soon after presented by the States to Marshal Conway, who carried it to his seat at Park Place, near Henley; but we shall resume the subjects in another place.

A few years afterwards, the French Revolution burst out in all its violence, and was soon after followed by an obstinate and destructive war, which lasted more than 20 years. In 1814, the Duke of Berry, made a short stay in this island on his return to France.

At the time of the death of Louis XVI. in 1793, the island was crowded with French emigrants, many of whom were persons of high rank and distinction, who had found here hospitality and protection from the daggers of the midnight assassin, and the lifted axe of the mockery of justice.

It is also to the honour of this island, that the persecuted, and distressed French clergy, were welcomed with open arms within its limits. Misfortune allays the venom of religious acrimony, and men are reminded that a common nature has imprescriptible claims to charity and humanity, which even superstition and intolerance cannot destroy. At one time four French prelates had made this island their temporary abode; the bishops of Bayeux, Dol, Treguier, and St. Paul de Léon. The first of these died here, and like many of his exiled countrymen, was buried in St. Saviour's Church-yard; but no stone or inscription points out his grave to posterity.

The deportment of that clergy, was mild, inoffensive, and pious, such as became their holy profession in a state of affliction and suffering. It was then computed that at one time the French emigrants, and clergy, amounted at least to 5,000.

The last event of a military nature, which has happened in Jersey, has been the construction of Fort Regent, on the Town Hill, an almost impregnable fortress, which at once protects the harbour, and commands the harbour, and Elizabeth Castle. The Duke of Somerset, during the reign of Edward VI., about 300 years ago, had intended to build a citadel upon that hill; but the design was soon after laid aside as impracticable, owing to the actual deficiency of the hill in the requisites of spring and well water. The hill, which was a common belonging to the Town of St. Helier, and on which Fort Regent is now built, was sold to Government in 1801, for £10,600, which has since been applied towards creating a fund for the paving and improvement of the town. That Fort, or rather citadel was begun in 1802, and was not completed till soon after the peace in 1815. The labour and the perseverance, which it required, have been immense, and it has been calculated, that the expenditure, which it occasioned, has not been much under a million sterling,

A fatal catastrophe had nearly happened during the building of this Citadel, which if it had not been prevented, would have involved the town in the same destruction. On the 4th of June, 1804, after the guns had been fired in honour of the King's birthday, the match which had been used for that purpose, and which had been apparently extinguished, was carried back to the powder magazine, from which it had been taken. The door was then locked up ; but soon after this, Lieutenant Lys, who was on duty at the signal post, and one Edward Touzel, a carpenter, who was then at work, observed some smoke coming through the key hole of the powder magazine. These two brave men with the assistance of William Penteney, a private of the 31st Regiment of Foot, who happened to be at hand, rushed to the door, and with their axes burst it open, while at every instant they expected an explosion of the magazine. As soon as they came in, they saw the match was on fire, and had already consumed part of the outer covering of a flannel bag containing a charge of powder for a great gun. If the match had not been immediately removed, it would have reached the powder in a few seconds, and then the whole of the magazine would have inevitably exploded. It is scarcely possible to calculate to what an extent the mischief might have been carried, if it had not been providentially averted, as above 100 barrels of gunpowder were then deposited in that store. The least that could have happened, would have been the demolition of part of the town, and the overwhelming of the inhabitants under its ruins. Thus did the presence of mind of those brave men, preserve the lives and properties of their countrymen, though at the imminent peril of their own.

The sensation which this heroic action excited was very great and every individual seemed to vie in gratitude to those persons, who had thus providentially been the instruments of such a signal preservation.   A large subscription was set on foot among the inhabitants for Touzel, to which the Lieutenant-Governor, Lieutenant-General Andrew Gordon, contributed Five pounds ; but whether as an encouragement to others to do the same, or as a compensation for any further claims on his patronage, is uncertain.   Lys, was promoted in his profession, and died a Major.   Penteney, had a pension of Twelve Pounds a-year from the States of Jersey, and died at a great age, only a few years ago.   Lys, and Touzel, in addition to their other rewards, received a gratuity of about 300 guineas each, from the States ; but the latter did not long enjoy those advantages, having died within a few years, in the flower of his age.

The three actors on that scene, being dead, it is impossible to elucidate after a lapse of forty years, any doubts which might now arise.   As George III., had near completed his 66th year, a royal salute had been fired in honour of his birth-day.   The question would then be, if it was likely, that the match without having been well extinguished would be carried back to the powder magazine. The name also of the individual, who locked up the store-room door, has not been recorded, nor is it known, what he might have said in his own justification.   In this state of things might it not be questioned whether there had been any real cause for alarm at all, and whether the coming of the smoke through the key hole might not have been imaginary ; or lastly, how could the smoke, if any, when smothered up in a confined store, and without any draft, have thus come out through the key hole ? Even if the match had been burning, would it not soon have been extinguished, when it had no vital air to support combustion, as in houses on fire, which do not burn very fiercely, till the doors have been opened, and given free admission to the external air.   But admitting that a match should be on fire in a store, those precautions are generally taken, that it might keep on burning without reaching the powder.   There must either have been an extraordinary negligence somewhere, or rather an unaccountable panic that seized the parties themselves, which made them to apprehend they had incurred a danger of the first magnitude. After it had passed over, they would still be inclined to persist in their belief, that it had been such, either through that general feeling of mankind, which causes individuals to think highly of their own merits, and to exaggerate the claims which may be due to their services. It afforded a further facility in doing this, that there were but few persons acquainted with the true state of things, and that those few were equally interested to increase their claims to remuneration by strongly impressing the public with a deep sense of the extreme danger to which they had been exposed, but which had been so happily averted by their intrepidity, and presence of mind. If therefore we admit that there was no collusion, and that the conduct of those persons was as meritorious as it has been represented, it cannot be denied, that after the favourable issue of that affair, the most was made of it to turn it to their private advantage, and that the excessive zeal of some persons to bias the public mind on that occasion, was not undeserving of reprehension. If after all, however, the rewards were more than adequate to the services, which had been rendered; the Acts of the States in which they were conveyed, and other documents of the kind, are fulsome and ridiculous.

CHAPTER X.

THE conflagration from which the Town of St. Helier, and the shipping in the Harbour, had so narrowly escaped, had been preceded the year before in the spring of 1803, by a measure, which though it did not threaten to be so immediately fatal, was even more to be lamented because of its effects, which were mischievous and permanent.

That measure is what is commonly called in Jersey the "Martial Law," which at that time caused such a general sansation throughout the island, that it excited open dissensions, and fostered the rankling of suppressed animosities, among those, who had made themselves prominent on that occasion. More than forty years have elapsed, since that ill-judged transaction; but a fair and impartial narrative of it, has not, as I apprehend, yet appeared. While an event that has caused any strong excitement is recent, it is next to impossible to collect the materials for a true and impartial history   The present generation knows but little about it, except from hearsay, which the farther it recedes from its original date, becomes imperfect, disfigured, and contradictory. Of the Thirty-six members of the States, who voted in that memorable sitting of their Assembly, not more than one or two remain, the rest with their virtues or imperfections, have found a refuge in the peace of the grave.   This silent rebuke given to the eagerness of human passions and to the vanity of all our pursuits, is of itself a motive to impartiality, and therefore I shall consider myself in the following Sketch, as one who writes about the departed beings of another age, who are to be remembered but so far as they supply the characters, which are to be delineated on the great canvass of history.

Every man in Jersey within the military age is obliged to serve in the ranks of the militia. Anciently they were trained in independent parochial companies, till the reign of Charles II., when all these were formed into five regiments of foot. They served without any pay, and till about 1780, Government did not even supply their clothing. As a privilege for all this, they are not liable to any courts-martial ; but all breaches of discipline must be referred to, and tried in the Royal Court of the Island, many of whose members are at the same time distinguished officers in the militia. The people are highly jealous, and justly too, about the preservation of that privilege. The introduction of Martial Law among them under any circumstances whatever, was therefore contemplated with aversion and alarm. They had before them in other countries, the summary rigour, which is inseparable from the exercise of Martial Law, and which is seldom adopted, except in cases of open disaffection or of an actual invasion. It had on that principle been proclaimed in Ireland a few years before ; but at this very time in 1803, when Great Britain, was threatened with a most formidable invasion from France, such a measure there was not even in contemplation. And why should a people, as loyal, and as high-spirited, as that of Great Britain, be subjected to so humiliating and unnecessary a coercion ?

At this period, Lieut.-General Andrew Gordon, happened to be Lieut.-Governor of Jersey. He had been appointed in 1795, and he held the office till his death in 1806. He was old and very infirm, but notwithstanding, he was still a skilful and indefatigable officer. But those eminent qualities were sullied by many faults. His ideas of military discipline were carried to an extreme, he was haughty, tyrannical, and overbearing, and of a difficult and uncourteous access ; impatient of contradiction, and still less disposed to listen to advice. A man in his high station was naturally surrounded by dependents, sycophants, and hungry expectants of patronage, whose only prospect of success was to please ; but that could be effected but by unconditional submission, and an almost servile acquiescence. Such was the Commander who determined upon subjecting the island to the operation of martial law, on the renewal of hostilities with France, in 1803, and when Great Britain and its several dependencies were threatened with a formidable invasion. It cannot be doubted that the General's motives were upright and well meant ; but the event proved that they were ill-judged, unpopular, and uncalled for by any particular necessity.

In this state of affairs, the Lieut.-Governor summoned the insular States to meet on Saturday, the 11th of June, 1803, as if to debate on a subject of the highest importance to the country. Of the several persons who were about his Excellency, it is not known that any was honest enough to remonstrate against the inexpediency of the intended measure. The States met, and the Lieutenant-Governor proposed to them to place the island under Martial Law. The members though evidently taken by surprise, had still the presence of mind to ask for an adjournment to consider the matter. As the States were then held with closed doors, and the reports of that sitting were not published, it is impossible at this distance of time to affirm what was actually urged in the debates, except that after much difficulty, the States were adjourned to the next day, a Sunday, a thing, unprecedented before, never since repeated, and a precipitation which actual circumstances did not then require.

As soon as the Lieutenant-Governor's intentions had transpired, a sudden panic, and indignation, spread with the velocity of the electric spark, through every part of the island. The feelings of the population were exasperated to the highest pitch, the greatest part of whom, crowded the next day into the town of St. Helier. As the members approached, they were surrounded by groups of their Constituents, who asked, solicited, prayed, and intreated that they would not forsake the cause of their country. An affecting instance occurred.—The Reverend John La Cloche, a venerable old man, and Rector of Trinity Parish, was riding slowly on, when he was accosted at a small distance from St. Helier, by several of his parishioners, some of whom affectionately reminded him to reflect on the important vote he was about to give, and conjured him not to stain by a pusillanimous conduct a long and honourable career. He was moved even unto tears, but made no answer, and in a short time voted to support the rights of his country. The Royal Square in front of the Court House, where the States were held, was crowded to excess, and never had there been the excitement of a more intense anxiety. There was neither noise, confusion, nor any tendency to insubordination manifested on the occasion. All seemed to wait in breathless expectation for the moment, which would announce the result of the debates, when all at once some of the Constables, threw up the windows, of the States' Hall, and waved their hands in exultation to the assembled multitude, that the Martial Law question had been negatived. There was instantly a universal burst of applause, which spread through every part of the town. Some of the unpopular members stood for a moment as they came out, as if intimidated at this manifestation, and as if uncertain how to proceed, when some of their political opponents, either with a good intention, or in derision at seeing their embarrassment, offered to conduct them safely home, which was gladly accepted, though perhaps, neither outrage, insult, or molestation, were ever intended.

The question was negatived by twenty-six, only ten having voted for the Martial Law, thus leaving a positive majority of sixteen.—All the Constables voted against the law.—The minority was composed of four jurats, and of six ecclesiastics, on the latter of whom the public odium principally fell. Although this passed off, without any open tumult, it made a permanent impression on the minds of the people. The most unwarrantable motives. were attributed to the minority and a general obloquy and contempt pursued them to the end of their lives. A whip and a halter, as the symbols of the most ignominous office were fastened to the gate in front of the Dean's parsonage, and some of the other clerical members were hung up in effigy, in their own Churchyards. Hence to have voted for the Martial Law, was on every occasion applied to others, as if to convey a term of the bitterest reproach. The States soon after offered a high reward to discover the authors of those lawless demonstrations, of the public feeling, but without success, and ridicule was in the next place, cast on this fruitless attempt to avenge the insults heaped upon those outraged members. Those acts, though unjustifiable in themselves, afford a striking lesson to men in public situations not to swerve from their duty, to court the favour of the intriguing or the influential.

It is usual in Jersey, that whenever a motion has been

negatived, to make no entry of it in the Books of the
States, and consequently a very scanty official memorial
of that Sunday sitting has been preserved. It seemed as
if the principal movers of that measure had wished to
throw a veil over it, and to bury it eventually in oblivion.
And now that they rest in the grave, well might it be forgotten, were it not desirable that a true and impartial
narrative of what had caused so much effervescence in the
public mind, at the time, should be offered to the present
generation.

Much might indeed be alleged to extenuate that popular
irritation. The people had not done anything to render
them deserving of such an animadversion, nor had they
like the united Irishmen a few years before laid themselves
open to the scourge of martial despotism, as the penalty of
their rebellion. Their ancestors had repelled the Constable
Du Guesclin from the walls of Mount Orgueil Castle, and
had prevailed over the intrigues of Margaret of Anjou, and
of the Count de Maulevrier. They were of the same stock
as that of those brave men, who with Sir George De Carteret defended their island to the last extremity against
the invading, and overwhelming forces of Cromwell, and
there were many still living, who had followed the gallant
Major Pierson in the defence of their country, when they
stood by him, when he closed his short but brilliant career
by victory, and an honourable death. It was therefore
extremely unwise and impolitic, to have pressed a measure
of this kind, when there was nothing in actual circumstances, which rendered its adoption necessary, and when
it was so offensive to a whole population, who were known
to be so decidedly loyal, and attached to their British
connection.

From 1804 to the present date, the Channel Islands have
been free from foreign hostilities, and indeed their history
offers but little of a striking or brilliant local nature, notwithstanding which this last period has been most rapidly
progressive in internal improvements and in the arts of
peace. The island of Jersey has now good roads that
intersect it in every quarter, its agriculture is flourishing,
and the fertility of its soil is such, that it yields an abun-
dance of produce, beyond what might be expected from
its very limited territory. St Helier has now a magnificent
harbour, and its vessels frequent the marts of every part
of the known world.

The Town of St. Helier, which 250 years ago, was but a dirty and insignificant sea-port, contains, now above 23,000 inhabitants, whose number, have about doubled during the last 20 years. The steam-navigation increases the facilities of communication with England, and encouraged to repair thither, strangers who are in quest of health, or of retirement have settled on its shores.

Nor let us forget that the English language has become generally understood among all classes, and that St. Helier has assumed the appearance of a new built, and flourishing town; but let us not forget that the most prominent feature of this period, has been the spread of a religious education indifferently to the mansions of the rich, and to the cottages of the poor, and that when England exults in the enlightenment of a true faith, the Channel Islands have not overlooked, nor neglected the opportunities among them for the diffusion of Christian truth.

It was at this bright period, when the British Empire had arrived at its highest degree of prosperity, and as a cumulation of our public felicity and exultation that Queen Victoria has visited the shores of the Norman Islands. The year 1846, will form for our posterity a kind of era in the history of our Island, to which they will often be proud to recur. It is therefore with that highly interesting event that we shall conclude this introductory Historical Sketch, and proceed to the other parts of this little work. It is however, proper to observe, that Her Majesty's Visit, is yet so recent, and so fully imprinted on the memories of most of our countrymen, that any further allusion to it, would be premature on our part, and that it has already been amply described by many able hands ; though if we were to express an opinion, we would recommend the Account which accompanies Ouless' Royal Album for which it was compiled, and the work itself dedicated by permission, to the Queen.

ARRIVAL OF HER MAJESTY AT MOUNT ORGUEIL CASTLE.

THE PICTORIAL GUIDE TO JERSEY.

PART II.

CHAPTER I.

First appearance of Jersey from the Sea.—Sea view of the scenery from St. Aubin's Bay.—The Sands, Elizabeth Castle and the Hermitage.—Ouless's Scenic Beauties.—Panoramic View of the Bay.—Town, and Harbour of St. Helier.—Fort Regent.—Coming into the Pier.—Affecting and striking objects on Landing.—Market Day. —Sabbath.

It was ten o'clock in the morning in the early part of the month of May. The weather was calm and serene, and not a cloud obscured the bright, and expanded azure of the heavens, till it was lost in the distant horizon, when the steamer which had left Southampton the evening before, had just turned round Noirmont Point, and was rapidly approaching with a fair breeze, the harbour and town of St. Helier. During the night, the wind had been contrary, and the water had been rather boisterous, which had then excited a sense of uncomfortableness, and even some sickness among many of the passengers. But now the diminished motion of the vessel, and the beautiful scenes that rose almost every moment successively in view, had banished every uneasy sensation, so that every one seemed anxiously disposed to enjoy the glowing prospects, which presented themselves in all that variety and profusion.

All seemed to have recovered from their late listlessness, and to be crowding upon deck, either to pace it up and down, or to sit in silent gaze and admiration of the many objects that rose on the different points of the neighbouring coast. The sight was lovely in the extreme. The smooth water was gleaming with the beams of the sun, that like infinite millions of sparks were reflected from

the surface.   Rising above the adjacent sea, there appeared a line of high land, which displayed all the appearances of wealth and fertility.   The fields were intermixed with groves and orchards, and the whole extent
was thickly set with elegant mansions, and here and
there, with farm-houses, or with small clusters of the
humble, but not less interesting cottages of the poor. The
tide had ebbed, and left dry a large extent of sand between
the water and the land.   The classical and the philoso-
phical mind could not help being forcibly struck with the
illusion, which brought back to recollection the arenas
and the gladiatorical shows of antiquity.   The passengers
could indeed see crowds of human beings moving along
those roads, but unlike to the sanguinary pastimes of ancient Rome, it was a quiet population moving in the avo-
cations of useful labour, or in the pursuits of innocent
recreation.   Add to this that the morning air was bracing
and refreshing, and that many imagined (though perhaps
it was after all nothing more than a delusion), that frequent
odours from the land were wafted to them over the waters,
and that before they landed, they had already had a fore-
taste of the delights of this fairy land.

These are the sensations which have been excited not
only in a few casual visitors, but in thousands on their
first approach to the coast of Jersey. This interesting sea
view must not however be understood to apply indiscri-
minately to every other part of the coast, though in general
all its bold, rocky, or low sandy shores, have each their own
particular beauties. The sea view to which we are now
exciting the attention of the reader is that which presents
itself to the stranger in a grand panoramic view of St.
Aubin's Bay, in a deep recess of which lies the town of
St. Helier. This view is said to bear a striking resemblance to that in the bay of Naples. This latter may indeed
be larger, and bring to the mind of the beholder a greater
number of classical recollections. But if St. Aubin's Bay
does not recall to remembrance the transactions of so many
ages, neither were its precincts ever polluted with so many
crimes. The mind that would turn aside with abhorrence
at the thoughts of the isle of Capri and the solitary haunts
of Tiberius, would dwell with pleasure on the bye-gone
times of the small Isle of St. Helier, and on the adjoining
rock of the Hermitage, once the scene of the penances

St Heller

and of the martyrdom of that holy man. The beauty of
the landscape which surrounds our bay more than com-
pensates, for the want of the cloudless blue sky of an
Italian climate. Or if our shores do not present the tombs
of such eminent poets as Virgilor Sannazaro, the fortress of
Elizabeth Castle, which commands St. Aubin's bay, was
once the residence of Lord Clarendon, where he wrote a
large part of his history, and where the poet Cowley found
a refuge from persecution. If the recollections of Elizabeth Castle, do not run over a long period, at least they
are pure and unstained. It was there that Charles II.
found twice an asylum, and it was there also that Sir
George De Carteret with a handful of the loyal inhabitants defended himself till the last extremity, and that
it had the glory of being the last Royalist fortress that
surrendered to Cromwell.

While the appearance of the sea and land was occasion-
ing those pleasing reflections, a passenger who had purchased a copy of Ouless's Scenic Beauties of Jersey at
Southampton, amused himself, and a few of his fellow
voyagers with turning over the lithographic prints in that
collection. Some of the originals appeared one after
another, as the steamer advanced into the Bay. Our little
party felt highly delighted in tracing the resemblance of
the lithography of Noirmont Point to its bleak and unpromising original. The eye was however soon after
refreshed by the neat little town of St. Aubin, with its fort
and harbour, the sea view of which was immensely improved by the delicious scenery of the contiguous amphitheatre of hills. A few minutes more brought the steamer
off the southern or back walls of Elizabeth Castle. The
eye had scarcely time to gaze on the external appearance
of that fortress, when the vessel was as it were by a sudden
enchantment transported into what is called the small road.
It is to this part that the chief of Mr. Ouless' views relates,
which is particularly remarkable for its striking likeness
to the beautiful originals. While we were thus amusing
ourselves with the work of the artist, and doing ample
justice to his taste and reflection, one of the passengers
informed us with an air of conscious satisfaction, that Mr.
Ouless was a native of Jersey, that the work with its il-
lustrations was an honour to the country, and that the
States of the island had so thought, who had voted him a

handsome gratuity.—An English passenger said with an arch smile that the love of country is never so attractive, as when its speaks the truth.

The panoramic view, which now presented itself was not very extensive, but it was enchanting in the extreme. On the west, as if to command the Bay, rose on a ledge of rocks, a little above the water, Elizabeth Castle, with all its appendages of walls, batteries, bastions, ramparts, gates, bridges, and towers, which proudly shewed, that it possessed ample means of defence, or of enforcing submission. But in a time of peace those defences were uncalled for, and the mind was better pleased to refer to its ancient history, and to elucidate the events of its early existence, when its precincts were yet the abode of a few scattered fishermen, or when it became subsequently the habitation of religious men, whose profession was to devote themselves to prayer, and to the practice of charity towards their fellow creatures.

The neat object that presents itself, is the Hermitage, at a few hundred yards distance from the Castle, from which it is separated at high water. The hermits' cell, which has survived the lapse of so many ages, and the desolating improvements of the scientific engineer, rises modestly a few feet above the top of the rock. It is a place still held high in the estimation of the inhabitants, from the tradition that almost a thousand years ago, it was the site of the seclusion of the holy man Helier, who suffered martyrdom for the Christian faith, and whose name has since been given to the flourishing town on the adjoining coast.

At the bottom of the Bay, and in front of the Castle, and the small road, a large number of Buildings, on a level with the water line a low sandy shore. This is the town of St. Helier, at whose extremity, and under the shelter of a projecting hill, a magnificent harbour has been constructed. This cannot fail to arrest immediately the attention of the stranger. Never did nature offer fewer facilities for a port, and never did art more completely triumph over the disadvantages of nature. The harbour of St. Helier did not exist before the reign of Charles II., and it seemed to be then more than problematical, whether it would ever be possible to form one there. Since that time it has been gradually formed, till by progressive improvements and accessions, its extensive piers inclose an

P. J. Ouless del.

Elisabeth-Castle

Château Elisabeth

H. Walter lith.

ample space to accommodate a large quantity of shipping, which now assign it a rank among the principal sea-ports of the United Kingdom.—But we shall resume the subject in another part of this publication.

The prospect, from this place, as observed before, is not very extensive. On the East, and rising immediately above the harbour, is the Town Hill, now Fort Regent, a citadel commanding the town, the harbour, and the neighbouring parts of the bay. The hill is isolated, or is rather connected by some slightly rising ground to a ridge of hills, which assuming a circular direction, incline to the westward, and after forming a semicircle terminate on the low sand beach, which faces the main entrance into Elizabeth Castle. The most western of those hills, and which bounds the town on that side, is of ill omened celebrity, and from time immemorial has been used as the ordinary place of execution; but its barren and unpromising surface has been inclosed of late years, and is now much improved by cultivation. The line which connects the two extremities of these hills, forms the low shore on which the town of St. Helier has since been built, and seems to have been originally but a beach of low sand hills, or an insalubrious marsh. Judging from the antiquities that were discovered on the Town Hill about sixt years ago, it must have been a highly sacred place, and much frequented by the Druids, —How strangely are things now diverted from their primitive uses! The Druids on the Town Hill have vanished to make room for a citadel, no vestiges of the ancient Abbey of St. Helier, are now to be found in the comparatively modern site of Elizabeth Castle: the very rock on which the little Hermitage stands has often been threatened to be levelled, that it might not interfere with the defences of its powerful neighbour, the swamp, and the naked sand hills have been replaced by an elegant and healthy town, and lastly that ill-omened hill, has now the most frequented road of communication with the western parishes of the island, made to run along the sides of its declivity!

In the mean time the steamer seemed to have glided into a smooth lake, surrounded on three of its sides by Elizabeth Castle, by Fort Regent, and by the town of St. Helier. It was now close to the entrance into the harbour, within which a large number of vessels lay at anchor, whose masts rose like a forest above the level of the piers,

which projected far out to sea, to increase the capacious-
ness of the port, and to afford the opportunity of a good
depth of water at full tide. For the conveniency of landing the passengers, she was run in alongside of the Victoria
Pier, when in a moment she was surrounded by boats,
sweeping with their oars on the surface to land those passengers, who on their side were not less eager to depart.
It was all haste, and almost confusion on deck, for every
one looked up and down to ascertain that all was right, so
that no part of the luggage might be mislaid through care-
lessness, or unintentionally left behind. On looking up-
wards, one could see the border of the contiguous North
Pier lined by a numerous assemblage of spectators. The
first thing that struck the voyagers, was that those spectators, had all of them, a decent and respectable appearance, and not at all inferior to those that one might meet
with in an English sea port town, and easily imagined
that he was either landing at Plymouth or at Southampton. Some of them had undoubtedly come there for
a morning walk, and with no other motive than a little
curiosity to see the passengers land, and to hear the news;
but many also had repaired thither, for the more laudable
purpose of welcoming their long absent friends, who after
escaping from various dangers, or having caused all the
apprehensions, which are always the consequence of any
protracted separation, were now safely restored to their
homes. It was truly interesting to behold the several
recognitions, which then actually took place. Many were
the nods, the waving of hands, and the salutations that
were interchanged from the deck of the steamer to the
edge of the pier, as the various individuals endeavoured to
attract the attention of those, who on their part were
looking for them with an equal degree of anxiety. There
were however, many on board, who were recognised by
the by-standers, with whom they were unconnected; but
as their arrival or not, was a matter of indifference, so did
it lead to no consequences. But as it was not so in every
case, so was there one, which was very striking. It was
that of an old weather-beaten captain in the merchant service, who after having been exposed to dangers in almost
every part of the world, had safely brought back his vessel
into the port of London, and was now on his way home to
meet the embraces of his wife and children. For five suc-

cessive packets his wife had come to see the landing of the
passengers, and had been disappointed.   She had not
however been discouraged, and had come there again.
She was a motherly kind of a woman, and of the middling
class, and was accompanied by her sons, two fine comely
lads.   It was not long before she recognised her husband
pacing the deck, and intensely surveying the long line of
spectators, who were standing on the pier.

A few minutes more had scarcely elapsed, when these
good people were seen forming a little group quite by
themselves, and so totally absorbed by their own feelings,
that they seemed to be unconscious of what was going on
in the surrounding crowd.   As to myself I could have
envied the delicious sensations which were then enjoyed by
that virtuous family.   It is indeed in the middling and in
the humble classes of life, that so much happiness and
sincerity is principally to be found.   Such a welcome
meeting had more of both, than is ever contained in the
boasted interviews of Kings and Princes, whom their fears
or their interest bring together under the semblance of
hollow friendship, or of dissembled reconciliation.   It was
in fact a kind of domestic triumph for that good woman
to lean again upon her husband's arm, and to lead him
back in the company of their mutual offspring, after so
long an absence and after so many dangers in safety to
their humble habitation.   Such a triumph as this, is one
of the highest endearments of domestic life, and affords
a far more real satisfaction, than ever fell to the lot of any
of the conquerors of antiquity, when they descended from
their triumphal car amid the deafening acclamations of
congregated thousands.

The scenes that now presented themselves to the passengers were indeed novel to many of them ; but they had
not that novelty, which is commonly felt on landing in a
foreign country.   It was pleasing to an Englishman to
observe, that the features, the manners, and the costume
of the people were the same as in England.   The language
itself of the by-standers, that great mark of national distinction was English, with the exception of a few strag-
glers of the lower orders, who addressed each other in the
old Norman French of the Island.

A large supply of porters was in attendance for the con-
veyance of the luggage of the passengers.   One was struck

with the civility and regularity of that sort of gentry, who
are so imposing and disorderly in other places. The good
order so remarkable here is owing to some excellent regulations of the insular States, and to the indefatigable
exertions of Captain Chevalier the present harbour-master
to carry them into effect.

Cards were then liberally slipped into the hands of the
passengers by different persons connected with the hotels
and other places of accommodation for travellers. As we
had been recommended in London to a respectable board-
ing house, we saw no reason to alter our choice. Several
carriages were in readiness at a few yards distance from
the landing place, where having hired one for ourselves
and our luggage, we got in, and ordered the driver where
to set us down. From the end of the Victoria Pier, it
was nearly a mile to our lodgings, in the town of which
we saw but little during our drive. We were received at
our new lodgings with all that attention and cordiality,
which nobody knows to practise better than the keeper
of an English hotel.

The house faces the Market, in Halkett Place, a name
which it derives from a former Lieut.-Governor, the brave,
and the generous minded Sir Colin Halkett. As it was
on a Saturday the street, and the market, were crowded
to excess ; much the same, as is the case in an English
country town, when a fair happens to be held. The country people in Jersey, whether for business or pleasure,
generally repair to St. Helier, on a Saturday, either to
transact business, as in the most central part of the island,
or where people may meet with each other, without being
at the trouble of going to each other's houses.

It was not long before the travellers, who were amused
with surveying this noisy and bustling scene were summoned to attend a comfortable and plentiful *déjeûner à la
fourchette*, which our more thrifty ancestors would have
called a most substantial dinner. Be that however as it
may, there was a profusion of all the good things which
the island could afford. After having laid such sure foundation, every former sensation of fatigue and exhaustion
disappeared, and every one, who had either been sick or
uneasy on the passage, was now revived with a general
flow of spirits. They had left London but so very few
hours before, that they could scarcely believe their senses,

how they could have been wafted over so soon to such a distance. The delusion was further kept up by the general appearance of the people, by the style of the buildings, by the cleanliness of the wide street in front, and by the comforts of the houses, which were evidently the same as are found everywhere in England.

As the day was already far advanced, it was not worth while to have undertaken any long excursion; but as the house was provided with an abundant supply of the local papers, which are published here in the English and French languages, they afforded ample amusement to the voyagers for some hours. It was not till the evening, that they sallied out for a ramble into some of the principal streets. The party consisted of persons who were all religiously inclined, and who were delighted to be informed that the Sabbath was kept here with as much holiness as in England. Under the impression of those feelings, they fully resolved to spend the next day, which was Sunday, either at their lodgings, in private devotion, or to go out to attend at some place of public worship. But as Elizabeth Castle, Fort Regent, and the Harbour of St. Helier, had already particularly attracted their attention during the latter part of the passage, it was agreed that a visit should be made to them on the Monday following. In the mean time they procured themselves the best Guide books and other publications of merit, which could furnish them with any necessary information.

CHAPTER II.

IN the forenoon of the next Monday, our travellers made a small excursion to visit the harbour of St. Helier. They had just been reading Ouless' explanations of his panoramic View of that harbour, and of the contiguous scenes, which they soon afterwards recognised on actual inspection to be correct.

The travellers were however informed, that very great improvements had lately taken place, and that a new Pier, which had been ordered to be built by the insular States, was but just finished. This had been projected to render the port more capacious, and to give it a greater depth of water, or rather, as it is a tide harbour, that it might enable vessels to come in at an earlier part of the tide. This has been accomplished by running out farther to sea, massy walls of granite constructed on scientific principles. The first stone of it was laid with great ceremony by the Lieutenant-Governor, the late Sir Edward Gibbs, accompanied by the insular States, who followed in procession with a large portion of the native population of the island, as well as of the British residents. This happened on the 29th of September, 1841. The expenditure has been very great when compared with the limited resources of the country. The funds were mostly raised by loan, secured on the produce of a small duty raised on spirits for home consumption, and on the harbour dues, which have become very considerable. These two sources of revenue are now estimated at more than £5,000 a-year each. Enormous as the debt incurred comparatively appears, those resources are sufficiently ample, to promise a gradual extinction, if properly administered. As to the work itself, it is not possible for us to pronounce any decided opinion. Whether the increase of wealth, and general prosperity of Jersey will be commensurate with the sanguine expectations of the projectors, time alone will show. Many persons are not without their apprehensions, that the commercial prosperity of the island, has already passed its acme, and that an increase of shipping, is but an increase of competition. The tonnage of every other part of the empire has also proportionally increased, and we have now to encounter the activity of rivals, which had never yet existed. The trade of the island, formerly found employment for its own shipping, or in other words, the Jersey shipowner and the merchant were united in the same person ; but now since the Jersey shipping has exceeded the demand for the freights required for its own trade, the owners have lost their independance, and have been compelled to look out for the employment of their vessels among strangers, and in other ports, whence have resulted many very serious losses, and other very grievous disappointments of some. If we are to trust some of the knowing ones, notwithstanding the harbour is flourishing and thronged with shipping, the gains of the shipowners have been diminishing for some years, and are now in the way of still further reduction.

The States had obtained an Order of Council, to enable them to construct a Wet Dock, at the upper end of the harbour, and along the line of quays, which runs parallel to the road called the Commercial Buildings. The spot had been carefully chosen, and independently of the public utility of a Wet Dock, it would have caused an immense improvement in the value of all the property in its immediate vicinity. It has however very unexpectedly happened that just as the excavation of the dock was going to be carried into effect, that a new plan has been brought forward, recommending to form that dock at the south end of the North Pier, but outside of it, and to be more capacious than the one, whose plan had been officially adopted. The new place therefore immediately became popular, and it is not unlikely that there is a large majority in its favour. The other party alleged the difficulty of retrograding after having obtained an Order of Council to sanction an Act of the States ; but the unyielding pertinacity of men's opinions, and the silent, but sternly disavowed workings of selfishness are more difficult to be overcome, than to obtain the repeal or the modification of an Order of Council.

The delay which has thus been incurred has given rise to further inquiry, so that from the turn that matters have taken, the question now to be decided seems to be whether it would be prudent to have a Wet Dock at all. The expense, it is estimated, would amount to above £200,000, and in that case, it may next be asked, whether it would not be highly rash and improvident to mortgage the revenue of the country to such an extent. It is true that a grant of Charles II., has appropriated that revenue towards the building of a Harbour; but it is evidently, a mistaken policy to give so much to one particular object however important it may be, and to suffer so many other improvements almost of an equal importance to be totally neglected.

If it should be asked what have the States done to improve or to decorate the country, what architectural monuments, they have reared, what churches have they built, what colleges have they founded, or what literary institutions have they fostered, the answer must be that of expressive silence, or it must be mixed with the bitter sarcasm, that they have done as little in any of those respects as any of their predecessors ever did in the darkest times of ignorance and poverty. It is true however that Jersey has within the last 50 years been astonishingly improved; but this in almost every instance has been effected by public subscription, or at the expense of public spirited, or even of privately interested individuals. Of course this observation does not apply to the sums, which the States have expended on roads, and on other works of a similar nature, which might be, more or less connected with the defence of the island.

This cursory view of the matter is suggested by an inspection of the harbour, and by the recollections of its history. Before this little work can be published, these very thoughts may have lost all their novelty and importance by a final decision, about which of the two plans is the more eligible. Be that decision however what it may, let us hope that whatever may be done, it will be for the advantage of the country, and that good sense, calm reflection, and a total absence of party feelings on the one hand, and selfishness on the other, will mark the final determination.

But though objections may be raised, and though vast sums of money may have been frequently squandered on this, as well as on some of the smaller harbours in Jersey, it must be owned that even that improvidence has not been without some advantages, were it only for the encouragement, which that expenditure gave to the working classes, and for that general spirit of enterprize, and of progressive improvement, which it kept alive.

The appearance of the harbour is highly pleasing and interesting to a stranger, for every part of it displays a degree of bustle, industry, and animation, which was never surpassed in any part of Great Britain. At a period like the present one, when navigation was making such rapid strides in England, it was but right that this small island should also have her share in the general race of improvement, and that when our neighbours and rivals at Granville, and at St. Malo, are doing so much to ameliorate their ports, we might also not be inferior to them in that respect.

The harbour of St. Helier, is likewise to be considered as the greatest artificial curiosity in the island. Nature seemed to have formed insurmountable obstacles to its creation, and where 150 years ago, there was scarcely a sheltering creek for fishing boats, there is now a crowded forest of masts, floating at high water in a magnificent bason. But what difficulties will not human industry and perseverance surmount! A deep and capacious harbour has at length been created out of the resources of Jersey herself, and without the aid of a single shilling from the British Government. It is to her harbours that Jersey is indebted for her present commercial wealth, and for the developement of the agricultural resources of her fertile soil. It is to this that we must trace the cause, which at this moment renders her the most thriving, the most commercial, and the most important of the Channel Islands.

This state of things has tended to increase a happy and enterprising population, which in its turn supplies a surplus of individuals, who crowd for employment in the merchant service. It is thus that the port becomes a nursery of seamen, to carry on the peaceful purposes of navigation, to the most distant regions of the earth, or to train a large proportion of the brave men, who might be wanted for the protection of the empire in time of war.

It is another consequence resulting from the great number of Jersey shipping, that many of those vessels now resort to the most distant ports, and that places which were formerly but barely known to the scientific geographer, figure frequently in Lloyd's List with the arrivals and departures of vessels belonging to this little island.—Add to this that a great number of vessels are also built in Jersey.

It has finally resulted from the operation of all those causes, that the port of St. Helier in its aggrandised state, is said to be now the " sixth" for tonnage and importance in the British dominions. This is indeed a singular distinction to have been acquired by the industry and the good fortune of a little island, only a few square leagues in extent, and of which it may indeed be. proud, since it makes it vie with the most striking efforts, and the eventual success of any maritime place, either in ancient or modern times.

Great as are the advantages of this port, and admirably calculated for the commerce of its flourishing town, it must be acknowledged that it is of difficult access, that the coasts of Jersey are rocky and dangerous, that the route from England to St. Helier, is circuitous, and that the latter cannot be approached, but with the greatest precaution. Some other stations, as Bouley Bay, on the North Coast, offer many local capabilities, and a shorter and easier communication with England. But the central position, as well as the beauty and the fertility of the adjoining district, evidently influenced the choice of having the town and the port at St. Helier.

As many of our readers may not be acquainted with the coast of Jersey, or have no books on the subject at hand, we close this chapter with the following Extract from DESSIOU's Channel Pilot. [London, 1805, page 72.]

This extract will supply an excellent explanation of Captain Martin White's, R.N., Chart of Jersey.

"Jersey is 3 leagues in length, from east to west, and 5 miles in breadth. Its N. W. point lies S. E. $\frac{1}{2}$ S. from St. Martin's Point, in Guernsey, about 5 leagues; its S. W. point 11 leagues N. by W. $\frac{1}{4}$ W. from St. Malo; and from the coast of Normandy, from 3 to 4 leagues. This island is surrounded with rocks, which render the access both difficult and dangerous.

"St. Helier is the principal town in Jersey; it is situated in the Bay of St. Aubin, almost in the middle of the southern side, and has the best road in the whole island, but yet dangerous on account of the numerous rocks, scattered round the entrance. The town and bay are defended by several batteries, but chiefly by Castle Elizabeth, built in the bay, on a large rock, to which you may go at low water. With northerly winds, you may anchor about a league without this bay, in 15 and 20 fathoms, clear of any danger from the rocks.

"The west side of Jersey forms another large bay, called St. Owen's Bay, wherein large vessels may anchor, in 12 and 15 fathoms of water, sheltered from easterly winds. Westward of this bay, about 1½ league, is a bank, called the Great Bank, extending 4 or 5 miles N. W. and S. E. where you may anchor in 12 fathoms.

"On the eastern part, is the Bay of St. Catherine, where the anchorage and the hold are good. St. Clement's Point, (the S. E. point of the island) is to the south of this road, and must not be approached nearer than a league, because of a ledge of rocks, called Banc de Violet, which runs from it towards the S.E.

"The tides set very strong among the rocks, and run the whole circuit of the compass in 12 hours.

"The two most remarkable ledges of rocks, on the north side of Jersey, are the Pater-nosters, and the Ecreho Rocks; the first lie about 2½ miles off the N. W. point, and stretch near a league east and west. The others are 6 miles from the N.E. point extending W. by N. and S.S.E. between 2 and 3 leagues. Both the ledges consist of a multitude of rocks, several of which are above water.

"To the south of Jersey, between 3 and 4 leagues S. by W. from St. Clement's Point, and about 6 N. by E. from Cape Frehel in Britany, are the Minquiers, a chain of rocks, 3 full leagues in length, E.N.E. and W.N.W. and above a league in breadth. They are very dangerous, for the stream sets right across them, from the west. The greatest part of these rocks are under water; those which shew themselves are called Les Maisons. The westernmost of the Minquiers, called La Derée, are always above water, and appear detached from the rest.

"Between 2 and 3 leagues from St. Clement's Point, S. by W. lies the Bank Grelets, about 4 miles E.N.E.

and W.N.W. and 2 miles broad, which are very dangerous.

"The tide, between the islands of Guernsey and the Caskets, sets on every point of the compass in 12 hours, (*i. e.*) on the full and change days, it sets, at half-past one o'clock, S. E. ; at three, East ; at half-past four, N.E. ; at six o'clock, North ; at half-past seven, N.W. ; nine o'clock, West; at half-past ten, S.W.; and at twelve, South."

CHAPTER III.

THE next morning as the weather continued to be fine,
our travellers left their lodgings to visit Elizabeth Castle,
the Hermitage, and Fort Regent. The road to the two
former places lies over a wide ridge of shingle, which has
been formed by the opposing tides, and is called the
Bridge. It is about a quarter of a mile long, and leaves
the communication open from the Castle, to the main land
at half-tide, twice in 24 hours. It is a place that ranks
high in the military annals of Jersey, and is still of much
importance from its having the command of the bay, and
because no invader, could approach the harbour and town
of St. Helier without having first passed within the range
of its guns.

The site of the Castle is of high antiquity, and is further remarkable for the various mutations it has experienced, about which we shall give a few particulars in
their proper places.

Mount Orgueil Castle at the East end of the island, had
been for ages deemed impregnable, and indeed it was so,
while the art of attacking fortified places was yet in its
infancy ; but as it is commanded by a lofty hill, which
nearly joins it, it soon became evident, that it could not
be defended against a regular battering train. At length
it was surveyed by some professional engineers during the
reign of Elizabeth, who made a report to her, of its utter
uselessness, as a place of defence. This happened in
1586, and from that date Mount Orgueil Castle was suf-

fered to decay, till it has become little more than a gigantic
pile of ruins, which is still deeply interesting by the recollections of its fallen greatness, and of the hostile bands,
who were so often repulsed from its walls.

In consequence of that survey it was then necessary to
look out for some more efficient means of defence by the
construction of another castle, which might be sufficiently
strong to arrest the progress of an invader. The small and
then deserted island of the Priory of St. Helier, in St.
Aubin's Bay was soon selected for that purpose, and measures taken by the Queen's Orders to carry it into effect.
The building of the new Castle was soon commenced, and
very properly received the name of its Royal Foundress :
but as it was built progressively and in detached parts,
and though it stood an obstinate siege in 1651, it was not
completely finished till the reign of Charles II., in 1670.
During all these progressive changes the ruins of the Abbey of St. Helier have so totally vanished, that not the
slightest vestige of them has descended to our times.

The principal entrance into this castle is at the North
end. The inclosure is a large one, as the walls surround
the whole of the small island, which is about a mile in
circumference. It would be superfluous to give any de-
tailed description of the several batteries, or of the
various spots, which have been particularly fortified to
prevent the approach of an enemy. That might indeed
claim the attention of the professional engineer, but could
afford no entertainment to the general reader. The main
guard stands on a rock, which rises singly within the castle,
and though it is not very elevated, it commands a view of
the whole of the place, and of the adjoining sea.

The castle has several barracks, stores, and other necessary buildings, but as these have the appearance of
private houses, it might be easily mistaken for a small
English town. In time of peace a very small garrison is
thought sufficient for its protection. The interest of the
place is diminished, from the spot being unknown, which
Charles II. and his brother James inhabited during their
temporary residence within the fortress. It is probable
however that it was in some one of those houses which were
since pulled down to make room for the present barracks.
The spot also where Clarendon wrote his history cannot
now be recognised ; but could it be found, it would be

more hallowed in the recollections of posterity, than because the exiled monarch had once resided there. Charles
found indeed an asylum in Jersey in his distress, and he
became in better times the benefactor of its loyal population.   It is not therefore surprising if his name has been
cherished with enthusiasm by an ardent and grateful people.   It is here indeed that tradition has handed him to
successive generations, as if he had been a hero, or a patriot king.   The stains with which his character is tar-
nished in English history are unknown here, and though
the memories of princes after they have once departed
-from the scenes of human existence, become the property
of history, and are treated with indifference, and even with
acrimony, the gratitude of Jersey forms a pleasing exception in the case of Charles II.

The Castle consists of two wards, of which the upper
one was built by Queen Elizabeth, and has received the
name of that Princess ; the lower ward is that of Charles
I. and was erected in the early part of his reign, and
Charles' Fort was added by Sir George Carteret during the
Civil Wars.   The Green, as it is now called, was taken
into the inclosure some years after the Restoration, in 1670,
and completed the walling-in of the whole of the island of
St. Helier.   It is not a regular fortification in the strict
sense of the word, as the walls, which form the inclosure,
have been obliged to follow the curves and the projections
of the ground, to prevent the possibility of an enemy being
ever able to form a lodgment near the walls.   The nearest
land from which the walls could be attacked, was on the
Town Hill at the distance of almost a mile, where batteries
might be erected.   But even if a practicable breach should
be effected, the assailants could not attempt it but at half-
tide, after a march of nearly a mile over the wet sands,
and having been exposed to the fire of the Castle.   If however they should find a protracted resistance, they would
be forced, in a few hours, to retreat, or else they would be
overwhelmed by the return of the Tide.—Thus far, one
might imagine that the Castle was impregnable, which is
not the fact, for it is so completely commanded by the
Town Hill and Gallows' Hill, that it could not be tenable
against the fire of an enemy, who had entrenched himself
upon those hills.

The importance of the Town Hill, was already felt during the siege in 1651, from the circumstance that the Parliamentarians had erected a battery upon it, from which they cannonaded the Castle for some time; but without effect, perhaps owing to want of skill, and to the great distance, till at length a shell having fallen into the powder magazine, and burst there, it occasioned an irreparable damage, in which 40 persons of the garrison perished. It may therefore be presumed, that if the Castle should be again exposed to siege, and had to struggle against a cannonade, it would in a very short time be compelled to surrender. It has been, therefore, to guard against such a perilous situation, that the Town Hill has been fortified, and that Fort Regent has been rendered the chief stronghold in the country.

The Armoury is the only place in the Castle, which is worth attracting the notice of the visitor, on account of a fragment of that shell, which caused so much mischief during the siege, having been preserved there. As no journal of the siege has come down to us, it cannot be now ascertained on what day that fatal shell fell. The siege lasted from the 23rd of October, 1651, to the 15th of December following. The shell was a 13 inch one, and 2 inches thick, being the largest size which was then in use. There is also another piece of curiosity kept in the Armoury, a large pair of antiquated military boots, said to have belonged to Charles II. They are in good preservation, and exactly correspond with those still observable in paintings, which relate to that period. But what an inconsistency in the human mind! The veneration paid by the Catholics to the relics of their Saints and holy men, is treated with derision by the Protestants, and yet we go with a kind of loyal superstition to handle an old piece of leather, because it had once been worn by a king of very equivocal character, and whom many historians have represented to have been a profligate and a tyrant.

After having taken this hasty survey of Elizabeth Castle, it may not be uninteresting to give some account of the small island upon which it is built.

There is a tradition that at some remote period, it had formed a part of the main island, from which it had suffered a disruption by some violent convulsion of nature. The fact is extremely probable; but in the absence of any positive historical record, it cannot be satisfactorily established. Se-

veral other parts of the coast of Jersey as well as of the
neighbouring continent discover frequent traces of the encroachments of the sea.   The formation of the Bay of St.
Michael in Normandy, and the separation of the isle of
Chausey, from the main land, took place according to the
learned Abbé Manet, during a violent storm about the year
600 of the Christian Æra.   If a conjecture could be safely
hazarded, it would be that the small island in question,
and as it now appears, was severed at that time from the
coast of Jersey.

If we admit therefore that previously to that time, the
external line of coast ran from the southern point of the
hill of St. Helier, to the present Hermitage, the walls of
Elizabeth Castle, and St. Aubin's Tower, the Bay, which
now is, would have then presented a large extent of a flat
and swampy shore, which when once that coast barrier
had been broken through, would freely receive the flowing
in of the tides, till in a few years the country would
assume the appearance, which it has since permanently
retained.   The light superficial soil would soon be washed
away by the waves, while successive storms would soon
cover the bottom with sands, or blow clouds of it towards
the shore, which would gradually accumulate into downs
and hillocks, till they had formed a new coast line.   It
adds weight to this supposition, that the water is shallow
between the castle and the main island, and that a large
extent of surface is still left uncovered by the tide.   It is
further observable that not far from Elizabeth Castle, there
are some beds of marle discoverable at low water, and
that quite recently, when some workmen were examining
the ground for laying the foundations of a Wet Dock, they
came to a bed of peat, which led at once to the inference
that this spot had been once a swamp.

In process of time this little island had assumed the
name of the holy martyr Helier, and it had been further
consecrated by its having been made the site of a celebrated Abbey.   When a grant from the then archbishop
of Rouen, united it to that of Cherbourg during the latter
part of the reign of Henry II., the marsh and mill of St.
Helier, are mentioned among its possessions.   That does
not however by any means lead to the inference that the
islet still made a part of the main land.

The very ruins of the Abbey of St. Helier have vanished

nor can its exact site, or even extent be now ascertained.
It is not however probable that the whole of the ground
had been built upon.   The constant tradition is that subsequently to the martyrdom of Helier, and in better times,
Guillaume de Hamon, a Norman noble founded this abbey,
as a sort of expiation for the guilt, which his pagan
ancestors had incurred in shedding the blood of that holy
martyr.   The date of that foundation is of the year 1125,
only seventeen years before that of the Abbey of the Vow,
at Cherbourg, by the Empress Maud, in 1142.   The
former Abbey on account of the circumstance which had
led to its foundation, was held in high veneration by the
inhabitants, and continued to flourish for a short time in a
separate and independent state, with regular Canons after
the rule of St. Augustine, till an unexpected occurrence
occasioned its decline. The Empress Maud, or Matilda, the
daughter and heiress of Henry I. having been overtaken
by a violent storm at sea, during her wars with King
Stephen, when on her return from England to Cherbourg,
vowed in her distress, that if it should please God to preserve her, she would sing a hymn in honour of the Virgin,
and found an abbey where she might land.   It is said that
the master of the vessel was the first to discover the shore,
and that on seeing it, he ran up to her in the exultation of
the moment calling out, " Sing, Queen, here is the land."
" *Chante Reyne, Vechy la terre.*   The words were omi-
nous.   The Abbey of Cherbourg, was named the Abbey
of the Vow, the name of *Chante Reyne,* was given to a
chapel, where the royal dame had landed, and the point
of land, which had been first seen by the pilot, has ever
since retained the appellation of Vechy.

Matilda had a particular affection for her Abbey, and
spared no efforts to promote its prosperity and to increase
its endowments.   The Abbey of St. Helier was then in a
flourishing state, and in high repute for the sanctity of its
inhabitants.   She sent, therefore, for its Abbot Robert, to
take charge of the newly founded Abbey of the Vow, and
Algar, the then Bishop of Coutances, sent her, at her
orders, a supply of Canons regular after the rule of St.
Augustine, for the supply of that establishment.

From that period of short-lived prosperity, the Abbey
of St. Helier began to decline.   It is true that her son,
Henry II., increased its revenues, by a donation of the

mill and marsh of St. Hèlier, but it was of little avail.
The partiality for Cherbourg still prevailed, and that
monarch was present at the consecration of the Abbey
Church in 1182, the ceremony of which was performed
during the vacancy of the See of Countances by Henry,
Bishop of Bayeux, by the Bishop of Avrances, and by
Joceline, Bishop of Bath and Wells.

It was at this time that Henry II. united the Abbey of
St. Helier, to that of the Vow at Cherbourg, on the ground,
that the two had not revenues sufficiently large to exist in
a separate state. This was done, as it was alleged, at the
solicitation of the Archbishop of Rouen, or rather as the
consequence of some intrigue to favor the Abbey of
Cherbourg. The allegation tends, however, to establish that the Abbey of St. Helier could not have been
richly endowed, or been thougth of much importance,
as otherwise that union would not have taken place
at the expense of the latter without some plausible pretence. It was, therefore, declared by a Royal Charter
of Incorporation, that Cherbourg should in future, be the
chief seat of that monastic establishment, or, in other
words, that St. Helier should yield the precedence to the
Abbey of the Vow, of which it was to become a priory,
and in reality, be but a humble appendage. Its establishment was limited to five resident regular canons, subject
to the regulations and the government of the Abbot of
Cherbourg, who was further intrusted with the administration of all the revenues. Such a grant was not only prejudicial to the Abbey, or rather Priory of St. Helier, but
in fact, it must have nearly annihilated it; and though it
has often been ostentatiously described by the local historians of Jersey, it scarcely ought to have been referred
to, unless it had been to prove, that in Catholic times,
Jersey had also its Monastic Establishments.

From that period nothing is known about the Priory of
St. Helier, except the probability that it lingered in obscurity among the great number of small Establishments
of the kind, which had then overspread the British dominions. The Alien Priories, or the ecclesiastical property
of Foreign Abbots was granted by the Pope to Henry VI.
That sort of property had, indeed, for a long time been
very insecure to the owners, so that the confiscation of it
could not have occasioned them any very serious, or un-

expected loss. Henry granted soon after with them the
other sources of his Royal Revenues in Jersey, to his
Uncle, the celebrated Duke of Bedford, on his being
appointed Lord of the Norman Islands.

It is therefore evident that those revenues were vested
in the Crown, but it is not altogether so plain, whether
those Priories, were, with the charge of their patrons
entirely stripped of their means of support, and consigned
to immediate ruin, or whether they were still allowed to
retain some pecuniary allowance. The latter would seem
to be the most likely supposition; but as no proofs of it
can be adduced as far as the Island is concerned, it must
be left as a matter of doubt, whether the Priory of St.
Helier was deserted by its Canons under Henry VI., or a
century later, when the Reformation was attended with
the suppression of all those Religious Communities. The
other lands and rents, which belonged to the Foreign Abbots, and which were not affected to the maintenances of
any of the Priories were involved in the Confiscation,
which immediately accrued to the Crown on the suppression of those Priories.

After it had been decided in 1586, that the site of the
Priory, should be that of the future Elizabeth Castle, the
ruinous buildings of the former were rapidly demolished
to make room for the exigencies of the latter. The Old
Abbey Church was, however, the only part which escaped
the general destruction, and continued to serve as a place
of worship for the garrison, till the siege in 1651. Some
vaults under it happened to be then used for a Powder-
magazine. During the bombardment, a shell, having fallen
into it, and burst there, it did infinite mischief, and killed
about 40 of the garrison by the explosion. The venerable
church was utterly ruined, and with its demolition, has
disappeared the very last vestige of the so-long famed,
Priory of St. Helier.

It is singular that the ruins of the Abbey of the Vow and
of its adjunct, the Priory of St. Helier, have met with the
same fate. The former has disappeared to make room for the
Naval Improvements at Cherbourg, and the former has not
the least remnant of itself left in the fortifications of Elizabeth Castle. What a melancholy reflection on the instability of all human affairs! How very justly did Juvenal
express it.

Quandoquidem data sunt ipsis quoque fata sepulchris.

CHAPTER IV.

Description of the Hermitage.—Martyrdom of St. Helier.—
Primitive Saints.—Antiquity of the ruined Hermitage.
—Town Hill, now Fort Regent.—Historical Sketch of
the Town Hill.—The South Hill.—Building of Fort
Regent.—Its present strength.—Magnificent View from
the Ramparts.—Cause of the want of public walks.—
Druidical remains discovered in levelling the hill in 1785.

THE next object, which meets the attention of the traveller, is the Hermitage of St. Helier. The legendary
tale of that holy man is extremely interesting, but the
details of it are scanty and want precision. It is a high
and solitary rock, at a small distance to the East of the
Castle, from which it is separated at high-water, and forms
the western entrance into the small road. Half-way up
the rock, and closely built into it, stands a small hermitage, which bears every internal mark of the most remote
antiquity. It is entirely built-up of small stones, in the
coarsest kind of masonry, something like that of the remnants of Grosnez Castle, which we shall have occasion to
mention in its proper place. This rocky habitation has
for ages been left desolate ; the doors, and the window of
the little room are gone ; but a cavity in the rock, scooped
to the size of a human body, plainly indicates the hermits'
bed of stone. The top of the rock contains a little garden,
whose bleak exposure commands an extensive prospect of
the distant horizon. There is a constant and uninterrupted tradition, that about a thousand years ago, a holy
and contemplative individual had chosen this spot for his
seclusion from the world, where, by his mortifications and
prayers, he might render himself worthy to inherit the joys
of heaven. It is not known whether Helier was the first
hermit, who had retired to that solitude, or whether he
was one out of a long succession of hermits. The island
had already been long converted to Christianity by the
Armorican Saints and other Missionaries ; but its population was rude, imperfectly civilized, and incapable of

much defence.   It was afterwards exposed to the depredations of the Norman pirates.   Those marauders were,
not only Pagans, but particularly hostile to the Christian
name.   It was during one of those predatory expeditions
that Helier fell into their hands, and was massacred.   But
the spirit of the times excited the sympathy of his countrymen, and the blood, which he had resolutely poured to
assert his religious faith, was considered as the test of
martyrdom, his anniversary was recorded in the Register
of the Cathedral of Coutances, as having happened on the
17th of July.   A perpetual veneration has attached to the
memory of that holy and celebrated man.   His hermitage
still nearly remains, after the lapse of so many ages, in the
same state that it was during the time of his seclusion.
He gave his name to the adjoining islet, and what was
probably then but a fishing village, has since grown into
the large and thriving town of St. Helier.

  Many of our readers are not aware that several of the
secondary order of Saints were not regularly canonised by
the Pope; but that they are indebted for their title to the
gratitude of posterity.   And one, who in modern times
would be esteemed among his neighbours as having been
disinterested, pious, and humane, was immediately acknowledged among his own immediate circle as a public benefactor, who had had something more than human in his
nature.   Religion did its part by enrolling him for a Saint,
and superstition either believed, or fondly imagined ficti-
tious miracles in support of its pleasing delusion.   Still,
if we admit this to have been the origin of most of the
local saints, a great deal that is praiseworthy will still
remain, and it will appear that for the most part, those
venerated personages, were neither over-heated zealots,
nor ignorant barbarians, but men laborious and unremitting
in their calling, and who went about doing good in their
generation.   These were indeed the Saints Vincent de
Paul, the Man of Ross, and the Howards of their times.
The claims of such individuals rest, indeed, on higher
grounds than those of heroes and statesmen, whose track
has been but too often marked by the sorrows and the desolation of their fellow-creatures.

  After having trodden with reverential awe on the stone
floor of the Hermitage, the next question that suggests
itself, is, whether or not it continued to be tenanted by a

succession of Hermits after the death of St. Helier. The night of ages has, however, left the answer involved in inextricable obscurity. It is not, however, to be supposed that such a hollowed cell, and within a few hundred yards of a religious house, should be suffered to continue untenanted, and to fall into decay. The Canons of the Priory would, therefore, take care that the hermit's place should be supplied, as often as a vacancy might happen, and minister to his little wants. If we assume, therefore, that this cell was occupied from the Martyrdom of St Helier in the Ninth Century, to the suppression of Monasteries at the Reformation, it leaves a period of about 600 years, during which time it attracted the devotions and the pilgrimages of the faithful, who resided either in the island, or in any of the neighbouring parts of the continent. Since that suppression it has now survived a dilapidation of 300 years; and rude, lowly, and simple as it is, it is now acknowledged to be the most ancient, the most interesting, and the most valued monument within this beautiful island. As far as relates to the sanctity of its situation, this Hermitage does not yield to the recollections attached to the gigantic and desolate ruins of Netley, of Tintern, or of Melrose.

After leaving the Hermitage, Fort Regent, or as it was anciently called, the Town Hill, presents itself. That elevated land forms the eastern boundary of St. Aubin's Bay, and under its shelter, as we have seen before, the artificial harbour of St. Helier, has been gradually constructed.

That ridge projects out to a small distance into the Bay, and consists of two hills, the North, and the South hills, which are connected at their northern extremity by a tract of comparatively low land to another ridge of hills that run up into the country. Those two hills formerly belonged to the Lord of the Manor, and to a part of the Commonalty of St. Helier, and were sold to Government about the year 1800. The town of St. Helier has since been improved with the interest arising from the purchase money, which trustees were empowered to invest in the British funds.

It had long been in contemplation to fortify those hills, as appears from the Rev. Mr. Falle's History of Jersey. After it had been ascertained that Mount Orgueil Castle was become untenable since the invention of Artillery, it became indispensable to construct some other place of defence. The Duke of Somerset, the Regent of Edward VI., and who was at the same time Governor of Jersey, projected to build a citadel on the Town Hill. The project was, however, laid aside, as the hill had no spring water, and it was doubtful, whether it would be possible to sink wells into it, through its immense mass of granite, of a sufficient depth to obtain an adequate supply. Perhaps many causes concurred to render the scheme abortive. The resources of the island were inadequate for such an undertaking, and it is equally probable, that the English Exchequer could not have then furnished the means which would be required. An Order of Council was indeed issued, in 1551, to fortify the Town Hill, and to effect several other objects; all which, for the time remained without effect. Some thirty years afterwards it was decided to fortify the islet of St. Helier, and nothwithstanding that, it was afterwards practically proved, during the siege of 1651, that Elizabeth Castle was commanded by the Town Hill, nothing was done to remedy that evil till 1787, when a citadel was ordered to be built on the South-hill. The work went on for some time, when it was suspended, and afterwards finally discontinued. That citadel, if it had ever been finished would have been of a very limited extent, and would have commanded the Castle and the Harbour, but could have done very little to protect the town in case of its being occupied by an enemy. The imperfect works are now but a mass of ruins, and can only be curious to ascertain the extent of the projected citadel. Some of the masonry, indeed, still remains, but the best part of the materials were subsequently removed, and used in the construction of Fort Regent.

The two hills are separated from each other by an opening between them of comparatively lower ground. The roads branch off through that opening, one that winds round the Fort into the Town, and the other which leads to the village of Havre-des-Pas.

This Southern hill is much smaller than the North hill. Professional men have differed in opinion as to the expediency of this attempt to fortify it, which took place soon after a visit of the Duke of Richmond, in 1786. The doubts expressed seem to have been answered in the negative, and it is now generally understood, that if that citadel had been finished, it would have interfered with the defences of Fort Regent. Its very existence there, would have obstructed the command which the batteries of the Fort would have had over the water. It is supposed that Government has decided upon its removal, and on the final levelling of the ground. In the mean time it has granted permission to carry off from it, all the rubbish which might be wanting for filling up, and completing the various works wanted, for the improvement of the Harbour of St. Helier. Large quarries are working round the hill, which have the effect of gradually diminishing its extent, and of raising and rendering inaccessible what remains.

We confine ourselves to facts without pretending to know, or even to conjecture what influenced the decision of Government. It was finally resolved to confine the fortifications to the north hill, and to erect a regular fortress on its summit. The works were begun in 1802, and were continued during the whole of the late war, and were not thoroughly completed till some years after the peace. They were carried on a large scale, almost gigantic efforts were made, a large well was excavated through the solid rock, to considerably below the level of the sea, and a copious and perennial supply of good water was secured to the garrison.

According to Mr. Plees, a contemporary historian of Jersey, the well is 233 feet deep. It has a diameter of fourteen feet at the surface, and is walled round; but after a short descent the width is reduced to nine feet, and the walling is discontinued, the rest of the well having been cut all the way through the live rock, which is in its whole depth, of the same quality. The well has generally from eighty to a hundred feet of very fine water, the daily produce of which is from six to eight thousand gallons.

The excavation was a most laborious undertaking, and necessarily attended with considerable expense; but the advantage of so large and constant a supply, must to a garrison be incalculable.

The interior of the citadel was also abundantly furnished with all the conveniences, which might be necessary for its defence in case of a siege, as well as with all the resources which might facilitate the efforts of art, courage, and experience to thwart the views of the enemy, and to protect effectually Elizabeth Castle, the harbour, and the town. It is said that those works did not cost much less than a million sterling. That sum could never have been supplied by the island, and therefore, could not have been raised, but from the united funds of a large empire. Nor would it, on the other hand, have been expended, if Government had not been decidedly convinced, of the loyalty of the inhabitants of the Channel Islands, and of their great naval and commercial importance. Those various fortifications have had the further effect of rendering their union with British almost indissoluble, as in case of an attack, they would hold out much longer than would be necessary to bring over a sufficient force from the protecting state to their relief. As long, therefore, as Britain shall maintain its naval superiority, the Channel Islands shall be safe, and their connection with the British Empire, as long as itself exists. For if ever England should lose the command of the seas, the Channel Islands would not only be severed from it; but the whole of its gigantic power, would fall to pieces, and be utterly annihilated.

It has been said that Fort Regent is nearly impregnable, and it is evident that without either cowardice, or surprise, it could not be taken but after a regular and protracted siege. No near approaches can be made to it, as the town lies between two hills, which are the nearest to it. Those again, are at a considerable distance, nor do they seem to be of a sufficient height to command Fort Regent.

Like Elizabeth, and Mount Orgueil Castle, it is open, at all times, to ordinary visitors; but if any persons were to be desirous of a more particular inspection of it, they would no doubt easily obtain a permission on application to the proper authorities. The view from the ramparts is magnificent in the extreme, large and well built town, lying as it were under one's feet, the Castle, the sands, St. Aubin's Bay, and the encircling amphitheatre of land; while the eastern side of the Fort presents, St. Clement's Bay with an extensive tract of low land, which is among the best cultivated, and the most fertile in Jersey. It is from that spot that on a clear day is seen rising above the distant horizon, the towers of the Cathedral of Coutances, and a wide extent of the coast of France, while in another direction, and almost level with the horizon, the dangerous rocks of the Minquiers stretch themselves for some leagues ever the sea, and lie about half-way between Jersey and St. Malo.

The Town Hill, previous to the erection of Fort Regent, had from time immemorial been used as a Common by the inhabitants, and the plateau at top, which had been levelled some years before for a parade, was very spacious. Though bleak and much exposed in rough weather, it was much resorted to for recreation at other times. On Sundays and on holidays, it was the best frequented walk of any in the neighbourhood of the Town. The sale of the hill was, therefore, attended with a privation to the inhabitants, to whom no compensation of the kind has yet been made by the Trustees of that purchase money. This was lost sight of, and the money was appropriated to what were then thought to be more pressing objects, the right of the Common was alienated, and a pleasant and salubrious walk was lost, a deficiency, which, after forty years has not yet been made up out of the ample fund, to which the town had just claims, that a part of it should be expended for that purpose. If, in the mean time, it excites the astonishment of strangers that such a thriving town as St. Helier, should be without a good public walk, or airy piece of land belonging to the community, and set apart for its recreation, it cannot be foreign to our purpose to indicate the true cause of it to our readers.

We have now seen how the small isle of St. Helier has been desecrated from the purposes of Religion, to which it had been so long devoted, and how the holy repose of a Monastery, has been exchanged for the vigilance, and the incessant discipline required for a military station. It remains now to trace, nearly the cause and effect, to the hill of St. Helier and to Fort Regent. The following is a summary of the circumstances.

The summit of the hill was very uneven, though generally speaking, it was a kind of table land, with a slope to the Southward, at the point where the two hills meet. After the invasion of 1781, large intrenchments had been thrown round this table land, which of course have all entirely disappeared after the construction of Fort Regent. On the highest point a beacon had been erected, to spread the warning of an invading enemy round the island; in other respects, the hill was bleak, barren, and rocky, and covered with stunted furze. This was the neglected state in which it lay, when it was resolved, in 1785, to level the uneven surface of the summit for a parade.   There was in this place a mound of earth, which, though apparently artificial, does not seem to have attracted any particular notice before.   On removing the soil and the rubbish, which was necessary to level it, the labourers discovered a *Poquelaye*, or Druidical Temple, composed of unhewn stones, and of a different construction from any that had hitherto been found in the island.   Many of those monuments have, indeed, been discovered at different times, and more are supposed to be concealed under similar eminences.   The nature of those *Poquelaye*, is intelligible, from their very derivation in Celtic : *poqué*, a heap, and *laye*, a stone.   It is said, that within the last 150 years, rather more than about 50 collections of those stones have been found in Jersey, some of which are still visible.   But the number is, considerably diminished, owing to the depredations of sacrilegious hands, who have carried away the stone, to be used for common purposes.   This great number of Druidical remains, seems to prove that the Druids gave the preference to insular situations, such as Mona, or Anglesey, for the erection of their temples, and that Jersey, at that remote period, which must have been prior to the conversion of the natives, in the fifth and sixth centuries, must have already possessed a very considerable population.

It is well known that the Romans persecuted the Druids, whose religion they held in the utmost abhorrence, on account of its supposed horrid and sanguinary rites.   Those proud conquerors were also, jealous of the influence which that unhallowed priesthood retained over the minds of the vanquished people.   The Druids, therefore, naturally endeavoured to avert the destruction, which was threatened to them and to their temples.   Of the approach of any imminent danger, they had, therefore, recourse to the expedient of withdrawing the latter from their reach and observation, by covering them with earth.   The concealment continued so long, that the very knowledge of their existence was gradually lost; and, as the country became afterwards Christian, the people were more desirous to forget than ; to retrace those seats of the Pagan superstitious of their ancestors.

This monument is supposed to be one of the most perfect

remains of Druidism found in any part of Europe, but, at the same time, it is much to be regretted that it has long ceased to be in the possession of the Island. It is known, however, to every one acquainted with its local history, that the island had been indebted to Marshal Conway, for very important services, and that the public gratitude could not do too much for such a personage. This may account for the enthusiasm, with which the States presented him with this valuable piece of antiquity; but it cannot entirely exculpate them in having voted away what might have been considered as inalienable, and as being the heirloom of their country. The conduct also of General Conway was injudicious, and such as he would have never adopted on mature reflection; for there was a sort of vandalism in thus availing himself of the lavish liberality of an improvident people. A parallel to this is found in modern times, in the curiosities, which Lord Elgin brought from Athens, and which now adorn the British Museum. It has been said, nevertheless, of late years, that this temple might still be restored to the island. It were to be wished that such a suggestion might be correct, and that it might ultimately be reconstructed in some appropriate situation, where it might permanently remain to be an honor to the country, and a gratification to the feelings of the inhabitants.

CHAPTER V.

OUR travellers returned to their lodgings well pleased with
their excursion, and in the course of the evening they
agreed to devote the next day to visit the town of St.
Helier. As the next morning happened to be fine, they
sallied out early, and were ultimately highly gratified
with their walk. As many parts of the town of St. Helier
have been already described in Ouless' Scenic Beauties,
and the explanations in that work were prepared by the
author of this Pictorial Guide, the following quotation,
which refers to a great part of the town, will not be unacceptable.

"The town and parish of St. Helier contain about
24,000 inhabitants, or one half of the population of Jersey,
The former was originally but a collection of low and
miserable thatched houses; during the government of Sir
Walter Raleigh, in 1601, it contained but a few inhabitants; nor was it paved till long afterwards, during the
reign of Charles II.

"The town began to increase, though slowly, after the
erection of the South Pier, till at the breaking out of the
French Revolution in 1789, when it might have contained
a population of between three or four thousand souls.
The subsequent increase of St. Helier is to be dated from
that period. The great number of emigrants and French
clergy, who sought refuge here, rendered additional buildings necessary, till in a few years the thatched and other

mean habitations, had totally disappeared.   The French
revolution was succeeded by the long wars, which did not
cease till 1816.   During all that time the island was free
from invasion, and enjoyed the advantages, which resulted
from the extraordinary expenditure incurred by a large
naval and military establishment.   The commerce of the
island was also visibly augmented ; but that prosperity
was still further advanced by the immense sums of money,
which the building of Fort Regent and of several barracks,
occasioned to be spent in the country.   It had been anticipated, that the return of peace would be attended with
a cessation of the prosperity, which flowed from Government sources ; but on the contrary, the trade and the
shipping, instead of having been affected by that circumstance, began to increase in a most extraordinary degree.
To such an extent has the commerce of this Island increased, that the States have expended a vast sum in the erection of a most magnificent Pier, which has just been completed by the Contractors Messrs. Le Gros and De La Mare.
It is a noble structure and has a most imposing appearance.
 " The limits of the town were much confined before
the French Revolution.—Halkett-place, the markets, and
the streets to the north of them, were nothing but meadows.   The same may be said of La Motte-street, and of
all the additions, which have been made to the east of the
house of Clement Hemery, Esq.   New-street, Don-street,
and David-place are all new additions.   In Bond-street,
the cattle fair, or market, was then held along the south
wall of the churchyard.   Beyond this and the sea there
was nothing but a barren waste of sand, except the ruins
of a fuller's mill, a small beach, and some offensive
slaughter-houses.   It was probably at this place, that the
few boats belonging to the town were secured before the
harbour had been constructed.   The same may be said of
the west, or lower end of the town ; for beyond Charing
Cross, which was the site of the insular prison, which has
since been demolished, scarcely a good house existed.
Sand-street, as its name imports, was then but a waste of
sand, over which were scattered some ruinous thatched
cottages of the rudest description.   All Saints' Chapel,
and the streets in its neighbourhood, did not then exist.
The same may be said in a great measure of several other
places in the skirts of the town, such as Great Union-road,

Rouge Bouillon, St. John's-road, the Coie, George Town, and Havre-des-Pas, which, instead of being large and flourishing suburbs, contained then but a few homely farm-houses. Add to this that most of the houses, which were standing at that time, having been rebuilt more lofty and capacious, contain now a larger number of inmates. The ground, which had been reserved to most of the houses for gardens and other purposes, has been, as it increased in value, sold for building. Even the sand, which had been embanked from the sea at the Esplanade, has been filled up, portioned out into several new streets, and now forms a considerable addition to the town in one of its most commercial and busy parts."

We make a few additional descriptions.—At the west-end of the town stands the Jersey Hospital, a very large and spacious mass of buildings. The establishment combines all the advantages of an English infirmary, a general poor-house for all the parishes in the island, an asylum for lunatics, and a refuge for the houseless and destitute, who have no settlement in the island. In a large country these form separate establishments; but that could not be done in a place of such narrow limits as Jersey, and on the other hand that combination does not seem to have been attended with inconvenience. The Hospital has a very imposing appearance on the outside, and its internal arrangements is highly praiseworthy for its cleanliness and the attentions paid to the wants and the little comforts of its destitute, sick, and aged inmates, which forcibly reminds one of the Alms' house of the Man of Ross.

> He feeds yon alms-house, neat, but void of state,
> Where age and want sit smiling at the gate,
> Him portion'd maids, apprentic'd orphans blest,
> The young who labour, and the old who rest.

The entrance to the Hospital is over a spacious inclosed lawn or garden, which is laid out in front, where the sober, and well-behaved poor are allowed to take exercise and recreation.

The Hospital was founded about a century ago, by the Executors of Mrs. Bartlett, of the town of St. Aubin. This munificent establishment rose from small beginnings, and has been since gradually increased to its present

state by subsequent benefactions. One of the wings was
.built about fifteen years ago, at the expense of the Executors of the late Charles Robin, Esq., of St. Aubin, who
appropriated part of it for a chapel, and further provided
an endowment of £30 a-year, towards the salary of a
Chaplain.

The superintendence of the Hospital belongs to the
States, whose power is again delegated to a managing
Committee chosen from their own body, who issue their
orders to the Chaplain, the Surgeon, the Master, and the
Matron of the establishment. There was till lately a considerable income belonging to the foundation, on which
the different parishes were entitled to place paupers free
of expense, each according as they are assessed to the
general rate of the island. The number of those foundation paupers, was, however, but small. The great body
of its inmates, now amounting to almost 350, consists of
destitute strangers, or of the widows and orphans of soldiers
and sailors, who had died, while they were stationed in
the island. These occasion a heavy expense, which is
defrayed by the island, according to the proportions to
which the different parishes are assessed.

This establishment met with a singular misfortune in
1783, Government having thought it necessary to increase
the military establishment in the Channel Islands towards
the end of the American war, and there not being sufficiency of barracks to accommodate all the troops, it became indispensable to have recourse to some expedients,
to avoid putting the inhabitants to the inconvenience of
having them quartered upon them. In consequence of
this, several private houses were hired for temporary barracks, and among the rest, the States were prevailed upon
to let the Hospital for that purpose. The poor were
drafted away into another residence, and the soldiers installed into a dwelling, which its founders had exclusively
appropriated for the relief of the indigent and the unfortunate, a measure of so equivocal a nature, that it cannot
be even palliated, but on the plea of extreme necessity.
The States yielded to the pressing solicitations of the Governor, and surrendered the Hospital; but, whether it
was the effect of deception, avarice, or imprudence, it was
not long before that measure was severely punished. About
a year afterwards, in 1783, the powder magazine, which

was kept there, caught fire, blew up, destroyed the building, and killed several persons on the spot. The Hospital then remained a scorched and uninhabitable ruin for some years, till at length the claims of the island having been taken into the consideration of the British Government, the States obtained a compensation for the destruction of the Hospital, which soon afterwards rose again from its ruins, and forms now the present building. The interruption lasted ten years, as it was not till 1793, that the poor were admitted again into their inheritance, which has not since ceased to prosper and to increase in reputation.

Farther to the West, and the very last object at the foot of the hill, is a large inclosed burying ground. It was purchased by the States in 1832, during the prevalence of the Cholera, and in that place were deposited most of the victims of that terrible pestilence. It has been mostly appropriated to the burial of strangers, and of other persons belonging to the lower classes of society. There are few or no monuments worth mentioning in this humble receptacle of the dead, where all is peace and solitude, and well beseems the memories of those who were unknown in their generation, and were consigned to this place but to be the sooner forgotten. The Jews have also a small unostentatious burying ground in the immediate vicinity.

All Saints' is a neat Chapel of Ease, belonging to the parish of St. Helier. It lies on the west side of the Parade, on an artificial mound, at a small distance from the Hospital, and was built about 12 years ago by subscription, to which the States munificently contributed £200. The minister is appointed by the Rector of St. Helier. The Chapel derives its name of All Saints' from its having been built on the site of a burying-ground, which was closed after the purchase of the new cemetery for strangers.

The Parade, in which All Saints' Chapel has been erected, was, as its name imports, made during the last war, for the convenience of exercising the troops. As the town of St. Helier had originally been built at the east end of the valley, and under the shelter of the Town Hill, a considerable track of ground at its western extremity, had been left as an unprofitable waste, overspread with sandy hillocks, and a copious growth of the sand-rush. It formed an extensive Common, and as there was then scarcely any demand for building, it had been left for ages unimproved, and exposed to fresh accumulations of sand, which every violent storm blew in directly over it from the sea. After this Common had been levelled, and converted into a Parade, and the Hospital and Jail had been fixed near it, the neighbourhood began to improve, the ground acquired a certain value, and some good houses were built. It then occurred, that the Parade would be well adapted for a public walk. The opinion prevailed, and the whole was laid out for that purpose in gravel walks, and planted with rows of ornamental trees, which have not, however, grown so rapidly as had been expected. That circumstance can be easily accounted for, as the substratum, in which they had been planted, was but a barren sand, incapable of supporting vegetation. The only remedy for this, and which has at length been adopted, would have been to fill the pits, in which they have been planted, with vegetable mould, in which the roots might have had room to expand. As the ground becomes sheltered and improved, the trees will also become more luxuriant, and as the neighbourhood will have a greater number of modern elegant houses, it may be easily anticipated, that at no very distant period, the parade will become a fashionable place of recreation, and afford to the inhabitants of St. Helier, a public walk, in every way worthy of their populous town.

The Jail adjoins the Hospital, and like it, the main entrance is from Gloucester Street. It is a strong and substantial modern edifice. It has a handsome and elegant appearance, and its front is of the most beautiful granite found in the island, and seems to be well calculated to promote the health, and to secure the safe custody of the prisoners. At a small distance it might be easily taken for a palace, or at least for some large public establishment. A house of correction was annexed to it a few years ago, and is subject to the same regulations as the jail.

In ancient times the King's Prison was in Mount Orgueil, from whence the prisoners were conducted almost five miles, to take their trial before the Royal Court at St. Helier's. There was a body of about 300 pike or javelin men, who were bound by the tenure of their estates, to attend the prisoners to their trial, and back again to the

Castle. That having been found to be attended with a great deal of inconvenience, it was resolved to build a jail at St. Helier, which was accordingly done under Charles II. Its site was in that part of the town, which is now called Charing Cross ; but having in its turn become ruinous and inconvenient, the States decided, that it could not be repaired, and ought to be demolished. That happened about thirty years ago, when the present jail was built to replace it, at an expense of above £16,000, and as the funds for that purpose had to be raised by loan, they form at this moment no inconsiderable part of the public debt of the island.

The internal administration of the prison may be comprised in a very short description. The maintenance of the prisoners was formerly at the charge of the Governor, as being the Grantee of the Royal Revenues in Jersey. As the Jailor was then, but poorly remunerated, he was allowed to sell drink without licence, principally for the accommodation of the debtors. That system has been done away with, within these few years, the maintenance of the establishment has been divided between the Governor and the States, and the Jailor, receives an adequate salary as a compensation for the loss of his license. The spirit of public economy, which has operated so many reforms in England, has extended its minute ramifications even to this establishment. The public executioner was an officer under the Crown, who was acknowledged as such in the King's Rent Roll, and was entitled to the pay of a common soldier, as well as to a suitable dwelling. But the office having been found expensive, and the salary burthensome, it was abolished, when all his emoluments reverted to the Crown. A part of the inferior duties, such as the flagellations of culprits, by sentence of the Royal Court, has been provided for by being assigned to the Turnkeys.

Formerly the Jail was without any spiritual provision, and it is only within these few years, that a Chaplain officiates in it, for though a Chapel had been built, it had been left untenanted. That duty has devolved to the Chaplain of the Hospital, who receives an additional salary from the States, to perform that charitable work.

The management of the Jail was formerly in the hands of a Committee of the States; but it is now entrusted to a

P.J. Quless del.

Place Royale.

C. Walter lith.

special Prison Board of six Members, at the head of whom are the Governor and the Bailly. Let it then be expected, that from the apparently pious, disinterested, and philanthropic character of some of those gentlemen, the public will not be disappointed in seeing that establishment flourish, as if it had passed under the administration of some modern Howard, of our own growth.

On leaving the Jail, and coming down Gloucester Street the traveller will find himself on the road, which runs parallel with the Esplanade. This is a large sea wall, which begins at the north end of the Harbour, and is carried in a direction parallel to the town for half-a-mile, which it is calculated to protect against the fury and encroachment of the waters. The road from St. Aubin, and from the western parishes, has been continued over this esplanade, till it joins the quays, and opens for those parishes a direct communication with every part of the Harbour, without the delay or inconvenience of traversing the town.

At the end of this esplanade, and in an open space, a weighing machine has been erected, the superintendant of which is appointed by the States.

We conclude with an extract from a letter, written the 6th July, 1837, by order of Lord John Russell, then Secretary of State, to the States of Jersey, relating to the projected alterations in the administration of the Jail, which have since been adopted :—

" Lord John Russell is glad to learn, from the report of the States, that they concur with him, in the propriety of paying the charge for an executioner, and the expenses of the transportation of felons to the Hulks, out of the Prison fund, and His Lordship has every reason to believe that the sum of £600 to be raised in equal parts, by a contribution of the King's Revenue, and by the States of the Island, will be amply sufficient to defray these charges, as well as the expenditure for the maintenance of the Prison, and every other charge connected with the management and safe custody of the prisoners. Should, however, from any unforeseen cause, the general expenses of the Prison exceed the sum of £600, Lord John Russell firmly believes that when the States witness the important advantages arising from an approved system of prison discipline, they will readily provide for such excess, and His Lordship hopes that upon a reconsideration of this point, the States will withdraw their opposition to this proposal.

" With respect to the observation of the States, on the composition of the Prison Board, Lord John Russell considers that six members will be sufficient, and His Lordship now proposes that the States nominate three members, one of the three to be the Bailiff, the remaining three being members ex-officio, viz., the Lieut.-Governor, the Sheriff and one of the King's Receivers.

" I am further directed by Lord John Russell to desire you will take the earliest opportunity of calling the attention of the States to the subject, and as Lord John Russell does not anticipate any further difficulties, His Lordship has no doubt the States will proceed forthwith to take such steps as may be necessary for improving the state of the Prison in the Island of Jersey, and every facility will be given by Dr. Hawkins, the Prison Inspector, to forward the desirable object.

" As soon as the Board is constituted they should proceed to prepare plans, which, however, must be submitted to the Secretary of State for approval.

" I have the honor to be, Sir,
" Your obedient Servant,
" F. MAULE.

" The Lieut.-Governor of Jersey."

CHAPTER VI.

Public Library.—Court House and Hall of the States.—
The Royal Square.—Statue of George II.—The Streets.
—The Theatre.—Markets, Prices, &c.

NEARLY in the centre of the town stands a plain brick
building, containing a large and valuable public library.
It is open to any person of respectability, who resides
in the Island, on the payment of a small and even inadequate subscription to the librarian. It contains many
scarce and high priced books, especially in Divinity and
Ecclesiastical History. Of late years, the States of the
Island have occasionally made liberal grants of money,
which have been applied to the purchase of the best Latin,
English, and French Classics. There is a Latin Inscription over the front door, which states, that this library
was founded by the Rev. Philip Falle, a native of Jersey,
Chaplain to William III , and a Prebendary of Durham,
who was then almost eighty years old. It may be worth
while to observe that Mr. Falle was the same person as
the honest and upright Historian of Jersey, whose work is
still held in such high estimation, that it has become in
some sort a text-book. Mr. Falle, lived to a very advanced age, and expired at his Rectory of Shenley, near
St. Alban's, in 1742, when he was almost a nonagenerian.

The Library received a large accession by the gift of
the books of the late Rev. Daniel Dumaresq, D.D., a
Canon of Salisbury, and also a native of Jersey. That
truly good and learned divine, lived also to be almost as
old as Mr. Falle, and terminated his earthly pilgrimage
for a blessed immortality in 1805.

The situation of the library, has been thought by many,
to be confined and inconvenient, and, therefore, suscepti-
ble of receiving considerable improvements. As the same
objections have long been made to the Court House, it has
been in contemplation to rebuild it, with the library annexed, in some more commodious situation ; but the execution of such a project, would require large sacrifices

from the resources of the country, and numerous other difficulties would have yet to be surmounted before this could
be carried into effect.   The librarian is in the nomination
of the States.   That situation which lately became vacant,
had been held for nearly a century, by the respectable
family of the Quesnels, through successive elections.   Mr.
John Falle is the newly elected Librarian.   He has the
house for a residence, but on the whole the office enjoys
but a slender remuneration.

The Court-house, or as it is called in French *La Cohue
Royale*, is built on the southern side of the Royal Square.
The word seems to have been derived from *coeo*, a Latin
word, which means to assemble, though ill nature has
often assigned it to *Cohue*, an old Norman word, which
means confusion.   Though the prisoners were formerly
detained in Mount Orgueil Castle, they were always
brought to St. Helier for trial, at least from the time that
any of the Records of that Court are extant, which do not
begin till the latter end of the reign of Henry VII.   The
business of the Court before that period could not have
been much ; but whether the Records previous to that
date have been lost, or whether some had been regularly
kept, it is not possible to determine.   The building is at
the charge of the Crown, and has been rebuilt more than
once.   The present edifice is a handsome one, and was
raised in the early part of the reign of George III.   It
has however undergone various expensive and ornamental
improvements, which have generally been paid for by the
States, out of the public funds of the island.   The interior
is distributed as well as circumstances can admit, the
entrance is into a spacious hall, which on Court days is
open to the public.   At the end of this hall, is the Court
itself, with the necessary accommodations for the magistrates, the men of business, and the different persons
more immediately interested in the proceedings.   A large
room on the first story, and fronting to the Royal Square,
has been fitted up for the meetings of the insular States,
with a handsome gallery, which has been erected at its
lower end, when only a few years ago, the debates were
thrown open to the curiosity of the public.   Adjoining to
the hall of the States are three other rooms, one appropriated to the keeping of the records of the Court and
States, another as a registry office for copies of all deeds

executed for the sale and transfer of real property, and a third reserved as a chamber for the Bailly and the Jurats, where they occasionally meet in private consultation.

This disposition of the Court house was originally sufficiently convenient, and quite adapted to the due transaction of official business. The change of times and circumstances has however occasioned many complaints about the inadequacy of that edifice. That part of the building, where the Court sits, is so much annoyed from the noise of carts in the adjoining street, that it often occasions an interruption to public business. Many plans have often been devised to remedy that inconvenience ; but the most effectual one would be to remove the Court to a less objectionable situation. Two things have however hitherto prevented it ; the former, the central situation of the Court for business, and the latter, the heavy expence which it would entail on the public.

In front of the Court House is what is now called the Royal Square, whose capacious area, was used for a market, till 1803. It was the spot where the short struggle of the 6th of January 1781, which ended in the triumph and the death of Peirson. It is now much frequented, particularly on Court days, as a kind of Exchange for the transaction of business, and as a public walk.

There is a statue, at the upper end of the Square which passes for one of George II., though doubts are entertained on the matter. It was given in exchange for permission to build against one of the ends of the Court House, by one Gosset, a Frenchman, in 1749. It was inaugurated with a good deal of ceremony by all the local authorities, civil, and military. The statue is gilt, and in a Roman dress, but is said to be of lead, with a new head which was fitted to its bust, when it was allowed to assume the name of George II. That head is not unlike those on the coins of that sovereign.

The streets were formerly narrow, and inconvenient, as in most of the old country towns, in England. Those streets have participated in the general increase of wealth, and the unceasing desire for improvement. Most of the old streets have been widened wherever it was practicable, the houses which lined them have been rebuilt, and the ground floors fitted up into elegant shops. There are few towns out of London, where the streets present a more

copious and splendid display at the shop windows. Of
the old streets, King Street is the best for trade, being the
great thoroughfare for the six western parishes, and as it
were a kind of London Strand in miniature. Halkett
Place is the most fashionable, the richest, and the handsomest of all the new streets ; Broad Street is also a wide
and open street, being almost as extensive as the Royal
Square. The town further, contains several modern ranges
of buildings or terraces, the principal of which are Gros-
venor Terrace, and the Crescent.

The latter was built not many years ago; in the centre
of which a neat and elegant Theatre was erected at the
same period. It is a beautiful edifice with a facade of
Doric pillars and an ornament to the town. The inside
of the Theatre, is fitted up with all the conveniences and
decorations usually required for such an establishment. It
is occasionally occupied by performers either from England,
or France. This theatre was built as a private speculation, and has long been thought to be a losing concern.
The taste for the drama was never very flourishing in
Jersey, and the religious spirit of the times has rendered
it of late years still more discouraging. A great deal has
been written against and in defence of the drama, and it is
not necessary to discuss a matter of the kind in this little
work. It may not however be amiss to observe, that what
the present age may have lost in accurate taste and in
sublimity of composition by the discouragement of the
drama, it has been more then compensated by the prevalence of the precepts of religion and morality.

The markets are the next object worth drawing the attention of strangers. There was formerly but one market,
which had been held from time immemorial in what is now
called the Royal Square, and cattle were sold along the
south wall of the outside of the Churchyard. The present
market was erected by the States, and opened in 1803.
There are now several markets, all of which are well supplied, and which have been subsequently opened at different times,—the vegetable and meat market, the fish
market, the foreign provisions' market, the fair, or cattle
market, and a market for pork and poultry, and is the
most roomy and elegant of all of them, with its principal
entrance into Halkett Place. The whole of the front of the
market to Halkett Place has a handsome iron balustrade.

While we are on the subject of the markets, many of our fair readers will not be sorry to have an average list of the prices of provisions. The Jersey pound is of sixteen ounces, but these are equal to seventeen and-a-half Avoirdupoise weight. All kinds of butcher's meat are from six-pence to seven-pence for the best cuts. From April to October, butter is on average from tenpence to one shilling and a penny per pound; but from October to March, it may be averaged at from one shilling and a penny, to one shilling and threepence per pound. Eggs in the summer months are about fivepence per dozen, and in winter 7d. Milk is carried to the houses, at 2d. a-quart. Bread according to quality; but the best seldom exceeds 1½d. and 2d. per pound. The island does not supply a sufficiency of corn, for its consumption, but the deficiency is made up by abundant importations from the North of Europe. Poultry mostly comes from France, and is very reasonable, a good goose from 2s. to 2s. 6d., and a turkey 5s. As to fruit and vegetables, they are abundant and cheap. That is also the case with fish, except at particular seasons. All kinds of groceries are not charged at half what they would cost in England. As to wines and spirits, the reduction is still more considerable. The very best Cognac Brandy, 7s. 6d. per gallon. Fine Brandy, 3s. 6d. per gallon. Pure Hollands, 3s. 6d. per gallon. Port Wine from 9s. to 18s. a dozen.—Finest Marsala, 8s. a dozen. Fine Sherries from 12s. to £1 4s. per dozen. But wherefore all this enumeration of the finest wines to tantalize and irritate the thirst of many of our readers? It is therefore best to conclude by recommending in the words of the Jersey, Wine, Spirit, and Porter Metropolitan Company, their superior Sparkling Champaign, at 36s. a dozen.

The day was now far advanced, our travellers after strolling a little longer, and amusing themselves with a peep at the different fine shops in Halkett Place, returned to their lodgings with a keen appetite, for the gratification of which, they found a copious repast spread before them, which argued well in favour of the good cheer and the salubrity of the Channel Islands.

CHAPTER VII.

Early conversion of Jersey to Christianity.—St. Magloire. —Pretextatus.—St. Helier the hermit.—Old insular Chapels.—Consecration of the Parish Churches.—Episcopal Jurisdiction.—St. Helier's Church.—Improvements of the Churchyard.—Monuments.—Maximilian Norreys. —Gertrude Amy.—Major Peirson.—De Rullecour.— Charles D'Auvergne.—Brigadier General Anquetil— Eulogy of the late Dean Dupré.—His French translation of the Dying Christian to his Soul.

AFTER having finished the Visit of the Town of St. Helier, and called the attention of the reader to some of the most prominent objects of interest or curiosity, we may conclude by devoting a few pages to the examination of the venerable Town Church of St. Helier, and of other edifices, which have been erected for the worship of God, as the wealth, the population, and the resources of the island increased.

The conversion of the Channel Islands to the Christian faith is of a very ancient date, and is most probably of a period anterior to the subversion of the Roman Empire in Gaul. It cannot be that Christianity should have spread through every part of the Empire, that a long list of martyrs, and of Christian writers should have flourished, and that it should have been the religion of the State and of the emperors, without its beneficial influence having extended to the coasts of Gaul, and to the islands of the neighbouring Ocean. It is barely possible that its progress might have been slow in those remote dependencies, and that a great part of the Druidical superstitions of the country might have remained. It is also not unlikely that the confusion occasioned by the invasions of the northern barbarians who overwhelmed the Roman Empire, might have eradicated much of the good seed, which had been sown in former ages; but it could not have been a complete subversion of the true religion, nor could it have effected a general restoration of paganism.

After the establishment of the Franks in Gaul, things continued in that state till the end of the sixth century. It was then that the primitive Christians, who had formerly found an asylum in Wales, in Cornwall, and in Ireland returned to reconvert Armorica, and the adjoining provinces of the Continent. Great numbers of the laity, were then flying from Britain from the ravages of the Saxons into Armorica, where they founded a new country, and gave it the name of the land of their forefathers. They were accompanied in their exile by several of the clergy, who carried before them the blessings of peace and civilisation to the benighted tribes of the earth. This accounts for so many British names of Saints being still to be found in the names of families, and of parishes, such as Pengelly, Tremalga, Trehonnais, St. Ouen, St. Samson, St. Budoc, St. Brieu, and Dinan. Some of those holy men settled in Jersey, and were abundantly successful in their mission. The honor of evangelising the Channel Islands belongs to St. Magloire, who had succeeded St. Samson in the see of Dol, which he resigned soon after, that he might devote himself to contemplation and to the propagation of the Gospel. He founded a convent in the Isle of Sark, and then came over to Jersey, where he settled and built a small chapel, near the site of the present Grammar School of St. Manlier. There he closed his mortal career in peace amid the blessings of a grateful and religious people. Sixty years after his death his body was removed by one of the Armorican princes to the Abbey of Lihou, near Dinan in Britany, where it remained till the invasions of the Normans. It was then finally transferred to Paris, where it gave its name to the splendid church of St. Bartholomew, and St. Magloire.

The generous efforts of that holy man were afterwards more fully developed by Pretextatus, who spent the last ten years of his life in Jersey. He had been Archbishop of Rouen in Neustria, from which he had been ejected through the violence, and the intrigues of Fredegunda, the Queen of Chilperic, one of the Kings of France. At last he was recalled to resume his high office, but he did not enjoy it long. The Queen sent an assassin, who cruelly murdered him in his church; the memory of the victim, was subsequently honoured as that of a martyr.

Another Christian Worthy, of a somewhat more recent

period, was St. Helier, the holy Hermit, and afterwards
the patron saint of the town, which bears his name. There
have been some doubts raised about the identity of that
holy martyr, and some having pretended, that it was the
same person as St. Hilary, the Bishop of Poictiers, while
others have sought to identify him with one of the com-
panions of St. Marcou, the apostle of the peninsula of the
Cotentin of which Jersey forms a part. Mr. Falle, the historian of Jersey, shows the futility of the former opinion, and
though the latter is supported by the authority of M. De
Gerville of Valognes, one of the most celebrated antiquaries
in France, I cannot persuade myself that his views are
accurate. "St. Helier," says he "n'était pas un hermite
"venu à Jersey, pour se cacher dans le creux d'un rocher,
"c'était un des compagnous de St. Marcou, apôtre du
"Cotentin, dont Jersey faisait partie. Il animait la mission
"de St. Magloire comme Pretextat là consommée."

There is no proof that St. Helier was not a hermit, and
a martyr, as he has been represented by the constant
tradition of so many ages, nor is there anything in the
legend to render it improbable. He chose the hollow of
a rock for his seclusion, and the broad expanse of heaven
for contemplation, circumstances, which have always
formed the favourite objects of the warm and enthusiastic
mind. The same eccentricity exists even now, though it
may show itself in many different ways. We may then
easily conceive that St. Helier was one of those vigorous
spirits, who wished to acquire a character for extraordinary
sanctity, and thought that the most effectual way to obtain
it was by the privations of solitude, and penance.

We may therefore assume that St. Helier, was a native
of Jersey, and that he devoted himself to an ascetic course
of life, which by its very singularity attracts the notice of
the vulgar ; and that his Christian fortitude was further
exposed to the bitter trial of falling into the hands of the
Norman pagans, who mercilessly put him to death. His
constancy in the faith, and his undaunted courage in suffering, excited the sympathy and the admiration of his
countrymen, who raised his memory to that of a martyr,
and a saint. There is no need to have recourse to either
extraordinary virtue or talents. Any ordinary person,
whose life had been so blameless, and his end so edifying,
would anywhere be equally respected, and his memory

not soon forgotten. This brings us to the building of a church, as near as could be to the seat of St. Helier's martyrdom ; which piety placed under his invocation.

It is well known that St. Helier is reported to have been the last built of the twelve parish churches in Jersey. For several ages after its conversion, the island was covered with a great number of small and unimportant Chapels. At a subsequent period the island was divided into parishes, and the small chapels have gradually disappeared, till at present that in St. Brelade's Churchyard is the only one remaining. There is a list of dates of the consecrations of the different Churches in Jersey, which are implicitly copied from one publication into another. Those dates are very ancient, and may be correct, but they are not extracted from the Livre Noir de Coutances, as commonly reported. That book was compiled in 1274, and the church of St. Helier, was not consecrated till 1341. M. De Gerville already mentioned, speaking of the " Livre Noir," says :—" Ma copie que j'ai eu tout le temps de " copier ;—L'écriture en est très lisible. Je puis certifier " que dans ce Cartulaire il n'y a pas un mot des préten- " dues consécrations des Eglises de Jersey, ni de celles " de Guernesey, ni des prétendus Evêques consacrant. " Les Evêques d'Avranches avaient des dîmes et fiefs " dans toutes les isles, mais il n'y eurent jamais de juris- " diction épiscopale." After this testimony very little importance can be attached to that list of dates and consecrations.

This is the place to say something of the episcopal jurisdiction established in these islands. They were annexed to Winchester by an Order of Elizabeth in 1565. This had been done before by a pretended Bull of Pope Alexander VI., in 1499. It is plain, however, that that Bull was never executed, and that arguments preponderate to induce a belief, that it was a fabrication of a date subsequent to the Reformation. The jurisdiction of the bishop of Winchester exists in fact, but the Catholics pretend, that no temporal authority, has a right to alter the limits of any diocese, and that even granting the Bull of Alexander VI., to be forged, the Bishop of Coutances still remains a dormant jurisdiction over the islands. So late as the close of the last century, that Bishop appointed a Vicar general for Jersey. At present however, the spiritual concerns of the Catholics in the Channel Islands are administered by the Bishop of Winchester.

The Church of St. Helier, has nothing to recommend it in point of architecture, or of situation. It is a plain and unassuming edifice, in character with the simplicity of the times, and the scanty resources of the island, when it was erected. Like many other old buildings of the kind, it has received many additions, and pretended improvements, which have disfigured it, and given it an appearance so totally different from the humility of its general plan. It has been sometimes contemplated to rebuild it, but that would meet with serious objections, on account of the expence, and because it would interfere with the graves and occasion the destruction of many of the monuments.

Another circumstance, which adds to the celebrity of a Christian Church, is when it has been the theatre of some great event, or when it contains the ashes of men who had been eminent for their virtues. Except the martyrdom of its venerated patron and the high respect spontaneously paid to such unyielding virtue, the Church of St. Helier, has nothing historical to recommend it to particular observation. The inside of the church has an awkward and grotesque appearance from an absurd affectation of modern ornaments and improvements. The churchyard having become inconveniently crowded with human remains, it was closed in 1827, and another supplied by the parish in its place. The stones and monuments were left standing, and consigned to the slowly wasting effects of time. After a lapse of twenty years, a great part of them has already crumbled to pieces, and most of the inscriptions on the stones are becoming illegible. The churchyard has however just undergone a thorough embellishment, and is likely to be made a more attractive spot, than could have ever been expected. It is intersected by a wide gravel walk, that runs all round the church, and the high circular blind wall, which formerly concealed it from the street, has been removed, to be replaced by an elegant, and massive iron balustrade. It is the work of Mr. Joseph Le Rossignol, a native artist, whose good taste and mechanical talent do honour to the island.

The Church has a great number of monuments, but some of them are for individuals, who had no other claims to remembrance than the gratitude of their executors to inscribe their names on marble. There are however some distinguished exceptions, one of Maximilian Norreys of Ryecote, near Oxford, and the other of Gertrude Enys, of Enys, near Truro, in Cornwall, who died here in child bed in 1647. The inscriptions on those monuments have been copied in the last edition of Falle's History, page 349.

There is another monument which no visitor either a native or stranger can ever approach but with feelings of the most profound admiration, and the liveliest sympathy. The gratitude of the States of the island caused a monument to be erected at the public expense to the memory of Major Peirson, that gallant officer, who so essentially contributed to their liberation from a French invasion. The monument, is ornamented with very appropriate sculptures, which came from the chisel of the elder Bacon, who died in 1798. There is also a very neat and elegant inscription, giving a concise but energetic account of the fall of the young hero.

It is seldom that the fall of an officer not higher in rank than Major Peirson, has excited such a general sensation. This was owing to many causes; the sympathy for the glorious fall of one so young, for the peculiarly embarrassing circumstances under which he was placed, and for the permanent consequences, which resulted from his victory. Cold indeed must be the heart, that is not warmed to something like rapture, when it reflects, that even at this moment, the inhabitants of Jersey are indebted to his heroism, that they are British subjects, and that in that quality they enjoy so many religious and political blessings. If the French had then obtained possession of the island, it is very doubtful, whether it would have been restored on the return of peace, or whether it would have been ever again wrested from that power.

The Baron de Rullecour, who commanded the French invasion, was buried in St. Helier's Churchyard, in front of the place, where now stands the monument of the late Nicholas Fiott, Esq., at about four or five yards distance, and opposite the great western door of the Church. Rullecour, is said to have been a tall and stout middle aged man.

Beneath the monument of Peirson, there is another of a more humble description, raised to the memory of the late Charles D'Auvergne, Esq., a native of this island, and

claiming attention from his having been the father of the
late Philip D'Auvergne, Esq., and Admiral in the British
Navy, and Duke of Bouillon, in the Netherlands.   His
Serene Highness was one of those few men, whose enlarged
views, and whose exalted character reflected the highest
honour on his country.   Brave, disinterested, and beneficent, he was ever ready to patronize the deserving, or to
relieve the unfortunate.   The close of his career was however chequered by misfortune and ingratitude.   He died
in London, in 1816.—But his countrymen.

> Ploravère suis non respondère favorem.
> Speratum meritis.—HORACE.

There are several other monuments the sculpture of
which will please and interest the visitor.—But pass we
over them to approach with reverential awe a humble
cenotaph dedicated to the memory of the late brave and
unfortunate Brigadier General Anquetil, who perished with
his army, in the disastrous retreat from Cabul, in 1842.
That distinguished officer was a native of this island, and
the modest tablet consecrated to his fame, has been at the
expense of the late Mr. Anquetil, an affectionate relation,
who was not even his heir.   It is in some sort a reflection
on the States of this island, when they have yearly some
thousands at their disposal, they have not yet found some
moderate sum to be laid out in bestowing a suitable monument to honour the memory of a lamented native and a
gallant soldier.

Not thus have acted our neighbours on the opposite
coast in the city of Avranches.   One of their fellow towns-
men General Valhubert, was slain in one of the battles of
Napoleon in Poland.   A colossal statue was erected by the
emperor to his memory, and it now forms one of the principal ornaments that decorate his native place.   This lesson
given by rivals, neighbours, and foreigners, ought to be
understood by the States, as a gentle hint to do something
of the kind themselves.

The late Dr. Edward Dupré, sometime Dean of this
island, died in 1823, and lies buried in the churchyard;
but no monument has been raised to him either there or
in the church.   That Reverend gentleman was at once an
elegant scholar, a poet, an eloquent preacher, and on the
whole one of the most talented men that the Channel

Islands ever produced. He was the translator of Popes'
Dying Christian to his Soul, into French, and it is the best
version of it, which has ever appeared in that language.
It has been often printed in French collections of Psalms
and hymns. It is very remarkable that it was selected for
the anthem, sung at his own funeral. That circumstance
made it doubly impressive, when applied to its lamented
translator, and the effect it 'seemed to produce on the
numerous assembly who attended on that melancholy occasion, has never been obliterated from the recollection of
him, who writes this article, and who then witnessed that
imposing ceremony. We close our observations with a
copy of that translation, to which we subjoin another of
the same in Latin Alcaics from the pen of the Rev. Edward
Durell, A.M., Rector of St. Saviour's, Jersey.*

I.

Feu sacré, pure Etincelle,
Sors de ta loge mortelle;
    Entre la crainte et le désir,
O joie, ô douleur de mourir ;
Cessez, angoisse, agonie ;
    Je meurs pour naître à la vie.

II.

Entends les Anges des Cieux
    Leur douce voix te reclame ;
Viens, chère Sœur, en ces lieux !
    Ah que sens-je ? je me pâme !
Mes sens.—Tout en moi s'endort.—
Dis-moi mon Ame, est-ce la mort ?

III.

Le monde s'enfuit, se retire !
Les Esprits Divins de leur lyre
    Font retentir le son.
Je pars, je m'élance à la gloire.
O sepulchre, où est ta victoire?
    Mort, où est ton aiguillon ?

Christianus Moriens ad Animam,
Ex Popio Latiné versus.—*Auctore Edvardo Durell, A.M.*

* *Le Chrétien mourant à son Ame*, translated from the
Dying Christian to his Soul of Pope by the late Very Rev.
Dr. Edward Dupré, sometime Dean of Jersey.

O Tu, mei Pars, te Genus Ætheris,
Sedem relinquens corporis, hinc fuge,
  Ignava, pallens, et morando
    Debilior, metuensque mortis.

O quantus angor! quamque mori juvat!—
Natura, motus sed cohibe graves,
  Ut liber ex omni tumultu,
    Dulce fruar meliore vita.

Audin' vocantes Te Superûm Choros
Leni susurro ? " Cara Soror, veni,
  " Quâ blanda terrarum relicto
  " Te vocat exilio voluptas."

Quid sensibus me languidioribus
Solvit ? Quid æger spiritus it foràs ?
  Clausique caligant ocelli ?—
    Nonne fateris id esse mortem ?

Terræ recedunt, dumque abeunt procul,
Immensa Cæli lux aperit domos,
  Auresque mulcentur per æthram
    Tot resonare lyras Piorum.

Vestrûm quis alas commodat, et regit
Cursum volando? jam citiùs vehor.
  O Mors, quid ultra vim moraris ?
    O Roge, quo tibi abit triumphus !

EDVARDUS DURELL,

VII. Id. Jun., M.DCCC.XL.

CHAPTER VIII.

Burial Ground of St. Helier.—New Rectory House.—Church of England Chapels.—St. Pauls.—St. James.—St. Marks. —All Saints.—Dissenting Chapels.—Roman Catholic Chapels.—Sir Colin Halkett's Road of Communication.

AFTER having left the church and its more immediate precincts, we are naturally led to inquire for the burying grounds substituted to the ancient churchyard. There are two, both of which are sufficiently spacious; the former at the eastern end of the town for the parishioners principally, and the latter at its western extremity, where the greater part of indigent strangers, and other poor persons are generally buried.

The Rectory house was formerly adjoining to the Churchyard wall, but the situation having been found confined and disagreeable, it was sold a few years ago by the competent authorities, and another good substantial modern dwelling, has been built on ground belonging to the living near St. Mark's Chapel. The changes, which have resulted from those causes, are understood to have been highly advantageous to the benefice.

The mother church, having through the increase of population become insufficient to accommodate its congregation, several Church of England Chapels have arisen in different parts of the town. Most of these have been built by shares, and subscriptions, the holders of which cannot fail to have been influenced by a becoming regard to the percentage to be derived for their money, as in any other trading concern. It is supposed that those chapels make in the first place a competent allowance for their ministers, and for other incidental expenses. The remainder is then left as a disposable fund, to be distributed in their proportions among the shareholders.

St. Pauls' in New Street, is the oldest of those Chapels, having been built in 1816. It occasioned an opposition of some years from the ecclesiastical authorities, but the Chapel Trustees, finally triumphed or at least tired out ·

their adversaries.   The service of the Church of England
has always been regularly performed in that Chapel, but to
this day it remains unconsecrated.   The Rev. S. M.
Richards is the present Minister.

St. James, at the east, and most fashionable end of the
town, was built in 1827, the property of which was also
invested among shareholders, with this exception however,
that matters were amicably arranged with the rector, and
that no interruptions were given to counteract the good
work intended to be effected by that holy edifice.   The
chapel is at this moment highly flourishing, and is the
largest and the handsomest place of worship belonging to
the Church of England in Jersey.

St. Mark's Chapel, or rather Church, has been built
about seven years, and is almost contiguous to the new
Rectory.   It has also been built on the share holding
system, which strangely connects the letting of pews with
the prosperity of a chapel, and ludicrously enough introduces the daily purposes of trade into the sacred and
disinterested concerns of religion.   The Rector of St. Helier nominates the minister.

All Saints, so called from having been erected on an
ancient burying ground, is by far the smallest of those
Chapels. It is a Chapel of ease to the Church of St. Helier, whose rector also nominates the minister.   It is a
neat and elegant little building. It differs from the other
Chapels, in that it was entirely built by private subscription, except a grant of £200, which it received from the
States.   Its erection cost about £1,000.   After deducting
the necessary expenses, the rent of the pews belongs to the
minister.   The late Dr. Hue, Dean of Jersey gave £500
about twelve years ago to accumulate in trust, till it would
amount at compound interest to £50 a-year, towards
forming an endowment for the minister.   He is appointed
by the Rector.

There are other chapels belonging to several sects of
dissenters as well as two belonging to the Catholics. Some
of these have numerous congregations especially the Wes-
leyans, and the Catholics.

It is only of late years that there have been any Roman
Catholic Chapels in Jersey.   The first stone of the English
one, was not laid till the autumn of 1841. It is a large
and beautiful chapel, in point of architecture, and its ex-

ternal and internal decorations may compete with any other place of worship in the island. It is supported almost entirely by the Catholic English and Irish residents, the lower class of the latter of whom are very numerous. It has been dedicated to St. Mary, and as well as the French Catholic Chapel, is under the spiritual administration of the Catholic Bishop of London. The Rev. Mr. Mc.Carthy is the officiating priest.

About the same time an unsuccessful Anabaptist Chapel in New Street having been offered for sale, it was purchased by the French Catholics, who having fitted it up according to their views gave it the name of St. Thomas. There are but few resident French Catholics, either of note or property, the greater part of them consisting principally of the humble and laborious class employed in procuring supplies of provisions for the markets. Be it said to their credit, that they are a quiet, sober, and parsimonious people, and seldom implicated in any of those offences, which so often bring the stranger from other countries in trouble. This chapel from the general poverty of its congregation is supposed not to be in affluent circumstances, and it is probable that the funds required about £1000 for its purchase, and for its adaption to the Roman Catholic worship. These were supplied by the liberality of some unknown private benefactors.

There is a Chapel in lower Halkett Place, belonging to the Calvinists, the Rev. Mr. Beodet is the present officiating Minister.—There are several other chapels in St. Helier as well as others scattered over the island ; but of too little importance to attract the notice of the stranger.

The last thing that we shall notice about St. Helier is the military road of communication, which Lieutenant-Governor Sir Colin Halkett caused to be made about twenty years ago. That able officer planned this road for marching troops, and conveying artillery between the eastern and western divisions of the island, without being obliged to march through the town. Another use was also intended, that in case the enemy should effect a landing, the retreating army might occupy that road, and form a cordon round St. Helier, which would effectually preserve it from being taken by surprise. This road begins at the eastern extremity of the town near Plaisance. a gentleman's seat, then joins near St. James Chapel, St.

Saviour's Road which it follows till Quatre Bras, where it strikes into the Trinity Road, after which keeping a westerly direction, and passing the village of Rouge Bouillon, it is carried across to meet the St. John's Road. It then descends rapidly into the suburbs of the town, and terminates where it joins the St. Aubin's Road, at a place commonly called Cheapside.

Sir Colin Halkett, had left this road unfinished from Plaisance to the sea in the *Grève d'Azette*. That road has been completed by the States at a considerable expense, and is a great improvement.

THE PICTURESQUE GUIDE TO JERSEY, &c.

PART III

CHAPTER I.

Introduction.—Sir Walter Raleigh's Government of Jersey. — Dr. Hooper, and the Climate.—Its equability.—General salubrity.—Exceptions.—Immoderate use of Spirituous Liquors.—High seasoned food.—The Cholera.—Jersey Farm-houses.—The Poor's-rate.—The Feudal System — Old Roads.—Official Visit of the Roads.—Timber and Corn Trade.

AFTER having given our travellers a succinct Historical Sketch of the Island, and a description of the present state of the Town, it now remains for us to conduct them into a few of the most interesting parts of the country. It is not to be expected, that a work of this kind can present much originality; the most that any new writer can do is to present scenes already well known in a more striking and attractive view, and to take notice of any changes, or improvements, which have been effected by the general progress of civilization, and the various favourable circumstances under which Jersey has been placed in modern times. It may be said to have remained nearly stationary from the reign of King John, in 1200, till the government of Sir Walter Raleigh, in 1601, the summer of which, he spent in Jersey, when, according to some memorials of his residence preserved in the proceedings of the insular States of that period, his administration was particularly active. The administration of that great and injured man was short, and his life belongs more to the History of England, than to ourselves; still it is with some sort of conscious pride, that the Jerseymen of the present day, reckon Sir

Walter Raleigh among the list of their Governors. From that period the island began to improve.—Its final conformity to the Church of England, was in the latter part of the reign of James I. and was favourable to the island, whose very misfortunes under Charles I, and the Protectorate, enlarged its intercourse with England. The subsequent wars with France, under the latter Bourbons, gradually developed its importance to Great Britain, and essentially contributed to the welfare of its inhabitants. For a true account of Jersey during that period, we refer the English reader to the Rev. Mr. Falle's history, and to his copious commentator, the Rev. Edward Durell. It is, however, since the French Revolution, in 1789, that the island has made such rapid strides in the scale of improvement, that not a year seems to have elapsed, without some signal increase in its prosperity. Well might M. Luchet, a literary foreigner, and a recent writer on Jersey, exclaim "That every thing seemed to be new, and to have been created within the last fifty years."

In giving a sketch of the rural parts of the island, we shall have recourse to the best local authorities, particularly to the late Edition of Falle's History, to Mr, Ouless' Scenic Beauties, and to the recently published *Souvenirs de Jersey*, by M. Luchet, a man, long distinguished for the brilliancy of his talents on a larger sphere, before the iron hand of judicial severity, had compelled him to seek for an asylum on our hospitable shores.

Before we enter upon our excursions through this beautiful island, it will be proper to say something about its climate. For the substance of our observations on this head, we are indebted to Dr. Hooper, a native of this island, and one of its respectable practitioners. That gentleman distinguished himself during the prevalence of the Cholera here, in 1832, and published an account of it afterwards.

The climate of Jersey owing to its situation, and to its small extent, is remarkably mild, but for the same reasons, it is also very damp. It has, therefore, been properly observed, that there will always be a nearer approach to an equality of temperature in a small island, than on the coasts of any neighbouring continent. The heat in Jersey never rises very high, and it is but seldom that it descends below the freezing point. It is, therefore, very seldom

that the winter is attended with any very severe falls of
snow, or with any continued frosts, and the summer is as
rarely parched up with droughts. Nowhere does nature
present a milder climate, and nowhere do the seasons afford
a great number of days, with the equable temperature of
spring. The mildness of the climate of Jersey, bears some
analogy to that of the West of England, whose coasts
forming a peninsula, have the advantage of being placed
between the British and the Bristol Channels. That is
particularly the case with Penzance the most westerly
town in Britain, where laurels and myrtles thrive in the
open air all the year round, and where geraniums and
other exotics may remain exposed to the weather as under
the genial suns of the South of Europe. The spring however in Jersey is a little warmer, and the winter rather
less cold, than in that favoured part of England, which is
situated in almost the same latitude. The progress of the
two seasons here, is therefore more perceptible, and better
regulated. As to our neighbours on the coast of France,
there is nothing in their climate which can compete with
those advantages. But notwithstanding the dampness of the
atmosphere of this happy isle, it has a great counteracting
evil, in the north east wind, which coming over a vast extent
of land, impregnated with the ice and snows of Siberia, pre-
vails during the months of March and April, and is productive of serious injury to the earlier fruit trees. It is keen
and withering, causes a disagreeable sensation of chilliness,
that contracts and dries up the skin. It may be said, indeed, to be the only inconvenience of that fine climate.
The winter may be tiresome from its monotony, because
it does not exhibit some of those phenomena of nature, which
are so strikingly displayed in other regions, but it does not
last long, and its appearance after autumn, is softened
down again into spring, as it were, unperceived. In December the trees still retain a portion of their verdure, and
in the March following, there is already a renewal of
vegetation. The old way of not beginning the new year
till the end of March, setting aside all astronomical reasons
for the present practice, was the best adapted, at least, to
European latitudes. Beginning the year with the 1st of
January, is to make winter the first of the seasons, when
it ought to be the last, which is preposterous, and contrary
to the acknowledged analogy, which it bears to the ex-

hausted functions of Nature, and to the decrepitude of Man.

The climate of Jersey is, therefore, delightful for nine or ten months in the year. Even the temperature of the winter months has nothing dangerous, or even inconvenient, provided one takes but the ordinary precautions, which are necessary to be taken everywhere, by the sick and the convalescent against all violent and sudden changes in the temperature. It is on that account, that a residence here is so strongly recommended by the medical advisers of patients, labouring under chronical affections, as that very mildness of the air, which might perhaps be too soft for persons in perfect health, wonderfully co-operates in the former case, with the efforts of nature and of art. That is a quality, which our climate participates in common, and to a certain extent, with the warmer parts of Europe. It is also the same with the rearing of some tropical plants, which in England cannot be raised but in a hot-house, but in Jersey will thrive in common green-houses, and may afterwards be transplanted in the open air. The climate is also particularly well adapted to the residence of invalids, who have returned from the East or West Indies. The transition is not so great for them, as returning at once to the cold climate of England, and there is no doubt, that many very valuable lives have been preserved by a temporary residence in Jersey, till such time as they could be seasoned to encounter without danger the cold and humid atmosphere of their native land.

We must not, however, suppose that the salubrity of Jersey exempts it from the frequency of diseases. The mortality among children and young persons is considerable. Rheumatic pains, affections of the lungs, and disorders of the digestive organs, are unhappily but too prevalent. But it would be unfair to suppose, that such a long catalogue of evils, should be attributed to the climate. Many causes, however, might be assigned as giving cause to the development of those diseases, which it is unnecessary any more than to indicate in a work of this kind. What strikes strangers on their first arrival, is the absurd manner in which young children are reared, sometimes with too much, and sometimes with too little clothing, and by alternately exposing them to the extremes of heat and cold. Among the children of the higher classes too much indulgence in their meat and drink is often fatal, or else it generates complaints, which lay foundations of irremediable evils in after life. It is true that many do not seem to be affected by this defective training, but is to be attributed to the native vigour of their constitution, which overcomes those obstacles. In the country, children among the lower classes are brought up to premature and excessive labour, which is often fatal, or the insufficiency of good and wholesome food, makes them incapable of ever arriving at their full growth and strength.

Another cause of disease, and perhaps the greatest of all in the Channel Islands, arises from the immoderate use of spirituous liquors. It is true that this evil is mostly prevalent among the lower classes, but the evil is neither the less serious, nor the less dangerous on that account. The taste for spirits is very evident in the town from the great number of public houses, whose glittering ensigns stare in the unwary stranger's face. The cheapness of spirits enables the labourer to form habits of intemperance, which soon exhaust his little earnings, to the destruction of his own comforts and to the ruin and starvation of his own family. That manner of life carries its punishment along with it, by the inevitable loss of health, and that tremulous stupid sottishness, which is the forerunner of death.

The better educated and more easy classes are disgusted with such beastly habits, and it requires no effort in them to avoid them; but are they themselves less liable to even greater reprehension ? What those wretches have swallowed in strong stimulants, they sip up in small glasses, and at a greater expence, in the long list of luscious beverages.

Another fruitful source of disease in Jersey is owing to the large quantity of pepper, and of other hot spices, which are consumed in cookery. M. Luchet, observes that Jersey consumes more pepper, cinnamon, nutmegs and ginger, than all Paris.

The abuse in the selection of a wholesome diet, is closely followed by a perversion of the resources of medicine. After having passed a day of twelve hours in concocting some indigestible food or other, the next morning is spent in getting rid of it by gentle operatives. Hence the Chemist becomes almost as indispensable to the existence of the

lounger, as the pastrycook; for the number of pills, which
some of those gentlemen swallow in the course of the year
is almost innumerable. Every chemist prepares medicines,
and when we say that he does it, we mean, that he not
only practises it, but that on an emergency, he can also
invent new medecines to suit the taste of his customers.
From such a taste, however, exclaims sarcastically the
ingenious M. Luchet, *the Lord deliver us though we find
fault with nobody !*

Notwithstanding these several exceptions, one may
safely assert that the island has no diseases, which are
endemial to it, and that it affords a most salubrious place
of residence. After having ravaged several other parts of
Europe, the cholera appeared there also in the summer of
1832 ; but it did not rage with any particular violence,
and the cases mostly occurred among the indigent and
intemperate strangers, the ill-fed, and the ill-clad, without
a comfortable, or a permanent home.

The moisture of the soil, which might be dangerous in
other places, is not so in Jersey, where it is absorbed by
the high state of cultivation, and leaves no superfluous
matter to be exhaled in noxious effluvia. This is appa-
rent at the very first glance, for never did a country present a finer picture of rural happines or of general health.
This fine country is interspersed with gentlemen's seats,
farm-houses, and cottages in every direction. These, for
the most part, have neither the ostentation of splendour,
nor the mean depression of poverty. Let the tourist have
but the curiosity to enter the farm-house of one of the
respectable yeomen who inhabits it. He will be received
with the cordial welcome and the simplicity of the Jerseymen of the good olden times. He will find the parlour
fitted up with neat chairs, carpet, tables, and perhaps
even with a pianoforte, as at St. Helier's. The kitchen
too, though a less showy apartment, has also its luxury
in the profusion of its conveniences. Everything shines
and has an air of satisfaction, and the eye as well as the
mind dwell with pleasure at the sight, of the parents and
the children, and even on their domestic animals. The
dress of the family is neat, but plain, and betrays no
symptoms either of poverty or of slovenliness.

The feudal system still exists, but it is little more than
nominal, and is dwindled down to be merely a certain

·description of private property. Those who are accustomed to the sight of the highest wealth contrasted with the most abject wretchedness as they are exhibited in large countries, would in vain look for the same in Jersey. Freedom and industry, have raised the great mass of the people above those mean circumstances, the cottage which the Jerseyman inhabits, is generally his own freehold, which the great sub-division of property, and the laws of the country, have given him particular facilities to acquire. It is not, however, that there are no paupers in Jersey, but that the number of them is comparatively rare, and confined to unavoidable misfortune, to the helplessness of infancy, or to the decrepitude of age. It is true that a heavy poor's-rate is yearly raised, to which every freeholder is assessed according to his means ; a large proportion of that rate, however, is absorbed in the relief of destitute strangers, who have no settlement in any of the insular parishes, and must be sent back to their own parishes, or be maintained at the charge of the public.

Before we begin our tour, it is right to say something about the roads. These are the ancient innumerable bye-roads and lanes, which lead into every part of the island and present inextricable labyrinths even to those natives, who are not perfectly acquainted with them. We would not therefore advise any stranger to entangle himself into any of those inextricable paths without a guide, however alluring, they may be in point of shade, of seclusion and of rural scenery. One might be inclined if fanciful to imagine, that those bye-roads had been formed either to bewilder pirates attempting to penetrate into the interior or to check the advance of French invaders at some distant period. Those roads are repaired by a statue duty as in England, to which every person is more, or less liable, according to the value of his property. They are subject to a high official visit, once a year at Midsummer, by the Jurats of the Royal Court, in the name of the Sovereign, and attended by the Viscount or High Sheriff. As this visit is attended with much unnecessary parade, and closes with a good dinner at the expense of the Crown, its usefulness has sometimes been questioned, or treated with illiberal ridicule. Dr. Shebbeare, one of the historians of Jersey has a witty passage about it, which has often been quoted, in which he says, that the Viscount makes a solemn visit

of those roads in the name of His Majesty, attended by the
Jurats, the Constables and their suite, mounted as he
wittily ex presses it, on his " viscountal horse with his viscountal staff of office, perpendicularly erected on the pummel of his viscountal saddle."

The plain meaning is, that the sheriff carries a rod of a
certain length on the pummel of his saddle, and that every
branch that touches it, and obstructs the free circulation
of air into the narrow road, is ordered to be cut, and the
owner is subjected to a small fine.   Certainly, there is
nothing either ludicrous or unbecoming in the procession.
The danger of incurring the fine has, however, considerably diminished of late years, by the indiscriminate level-
ing of hedge rows, and the destruction of timber.   That is
done, as it is said, to throw the ground more open, and to
render it more favorable to the growth of corn ; though by
a strange anomaly, the home consumption of Jersey is
supplied from the Baltic.   It is always an injury to any
country to deprive it of too much of its wood, as it is a
loss which can be effected in a few hours, but cannot be
repaired but by the slow and progressive lapse of years.
It is sacrificing too much to the produce of grain,
and it is, therefore, an error.   The soil of Jersey is
adapted to the cultivation of fruits, and of vegetables ;
for nature formed there a garden, and not an arable
district.

The fact is, however, that the Channel Islands have the
privilege of exporting their corn to England duty free, to be
sold there again at the current price.   These exportations,
however, do not amount to any large quantity.   The Jersey
corn would not suffice for one fourth of what is needed for its
home consumption, which is made up from the Baltic and
from other countries, which can supply that commodity at a
cheaper rate.   The English farmers took umbrage at this
privilege, and endeavoured to induce Parliament to annul
that privilege in 1835.   They failed, however, and an Act,
subsequently passed by the insular States, to render all
fraud impossible, has removed the very pretence for any
prohibition of the kind.   Formerly the beverage of the
natives was their own cider, but since they have sent their
cider and apples to England, the consumption of spirits
has increased in proportion.   The cider which remains at
home, is that which would not repay the expense of

exportation. In consequence of that erroneous policy, many orchards have been destroyed, and luxuriant crops of corn now ripen, where not many years ago, the apple and the pear threw out their rich blossoms in the spring.

CHAPTER II.

THE military roads are the other sort of communication,
and are also of a more recent origin. The first of them,
the Grouville, or Don Road, was formed about the year
1808, and derives its name from its founder, the late Sir
George Don, the then Lieutenant Governor of the Island.
He had a great deal of opposition to encounter, which he
finally overcame by his moderation and his perseverance.
There are now several of those roads, all of them beginning at St. Helier, and communicating with each other.
Those roads have the appearance of English Turnpike
Roads, except in the essential particular that they are all
toll free, because from their having been originally con-

---

* The Compositor had made the following curious mistake in
the heading of this Chapter, where instead of reading—" Pro-
secuted in the Dean's Court,"—he made of it—" Prosecutable
in the Devil's Cave."

TYPOGRAPHICAL ERROR—AN EPIGRAM.

Sometimes it happens that a lucky hit,
Cuts deeper than the most sarcastic wit.—
The Canon made 'gainst witch and wizard means,
That solemn jurisdiction is the Dean's.—
Another sense the compositor gave ;
To prosecute them in the Devil's cave.

structed by the States, they are still maintained out of the general funds of the island.

The soil is good and fruitful, though generally light. In some of the valleys, however, one may find vegetable earth to a very considerable depth. The slopes of the hills, which formerly were covered with broom and furze, have been brought into cultivation, especially such as have an exposure to the South. The general declivity of the ground is from North to South, which presents, by far, the best exposure to the rays of the sun. The most elevated point is Mont Mado, on the North coast, and in the parish of St. John, where it is above 400 feet above the level of the sea. It consists of a mass of granite, or rather of sienite, of a superb grain, and of an extreme hardness. The lowest point is St. Aubin's Bay, where the two towns of St. Helier and St. Aubin at each extremity, seem to look at each other, the former as a queen city, and the latter as its humble vassal.

The lowlands which extend from St. Helier to Mount Orgueil Castle, near the circuitous road through St. Clement and Grouville parishes, and supposed to be the best in the island. It will be in that direction that we shall first conduct our Tourist.—We leave St. Helier near the Theatre, pass Plaisance, the elegant seat of J. W. Dupré, Esq., leaving the large suburb of George Town on the left, and going down a good road, we soon reach the sea-beach, where there is a commodious bathing establishment. on what is called the Grève d'Azette. There are always kept here a certain number of bathing machines in readiness. The accomodations are elegant, and comfortable, and the charges reasonable.

Above the baths, and parallel with the coast, runs the military road to St. Clement. At some distance from the road, on a rising ground, and nearly embosomed in extensive plantations, rises the superb mansion of Bagatelle. It commands a most extensive prospect. It has often changed its owners. It was the residence of the late Duke of Bouillon, then of Sir Thomas Le Breton, and is now that of Francis Godfray, Esq., an eminent Advocate of the Royal Court of Jersey. Such mutabilities do a few years produce in the tide of human affairs, that well may the philosopher exclaim, " That life has all the semblance of a dream !"—A little farther on we come to a large piece

E

of water, which from its oblong shape is not improperly
called Saumarez' Canal. It seems to have been originally
intended to drain off the waters of the adjoining swamp,
and to have afterwards answered the double purpose of
being as an ornament and a fish pond to the Manor of
Saumarez, close to which it extends. Some ancient recollections attach to that venerable place. It was, for a
long time, the seat of the eldest branch of the Dumaresqs,
one of whom was Henry Dumaresq, the republican, and
the adversary of Sir George Carteret. It was also the
property of Philip Dumaresq, whose Map of Jersey, is
prefixed to the Second Edition of Falle's History. He
wrote a treatise of great merit on the state of Jersey,
which, was presented to James II., in 1635. An avenue
of hardy weather-beaten oaks, formerly led to the Seig-
norial Mansion, and seemed to have resisted for centuries,
the sweeping storms that came rushing upon them from
the neighbouring sea. The oaks too have experienced the
vicissitudes of their ancient owners. They have been
felled, and they are gone.

After passing the avenue, an old road, perfectly shaded
by trees, and interspersed with several farm houses takes
the direction of the coast, at a small distance from which,
and in the middle of a field is to be found the Witches'
Rock, more commonly called Rocbert. Some of the good
people still aver that his Satanic Majesty, in one of his
nocturnal visits, left the vestiges of his cloven feet deeply
imprinted in the solid rock. It was there that in the days
of our grandmothers, the neighbouring wizards and witches
met to celebrate their sabbath. The belief in sorcery is
disappearing very fast, and the fear of the mischiefs which
its vengeance might occasion, has given way to derision
and contempt.

Well might the scoffer sneer at the ignorance and cruelty
of priestly superstition, when he is told, that the existence
of witchcraft is still acknowledged to exist in Jersey, and
that by the Canons of its Ecclesiastical Court,—it comes
within the Dean's Jurisdiction. It is, indeed, become a
dead letter, but there is always danger, as long as a law is
suffered to remain unrepealed, especially when in the
hands of a tribunal that pretends to be distinct from the
civil power, and which if ever directed by tyrants or fana-
tics, might be fatal to the peace of individuals, and to the

interests of society.—There is a vain and superstitious belief that no human force could remove the rock from its
present situation.   That will certainly be the case, till
some bold projector has the audacity to quarry it away in
spite of witchcraft, for the purpose of some impious speculation.

The sea appears again from this place, and at low water,
it uncovers an immense extent of low rocks, enough to impress the soul with horror.   On the right is the small
island of La Motte, containing about half an acre of land.
Its neighbourhood is noted for shipwrecks : but a little farther out to sea, and on a rock that the sea never covers, is
the tower of Icho, to defend the Bay, and still farther out, at
some miles distance, Seymour Tower seems to rise from
the waves, near which, the Baron de Rullecourt and his
French invaders, landed in 1781.   The path which lines
the coast of that terrific panorama, leads, in a few minutes,
the tourist to the village of Pontac, a place of fashionable
resort for convalescents, and for the amusements of many
a pic-nic.   There is an improbable tradition that Charles
II, landed at this place.   That Prince landed near Elizabeth Castle, and was attended by a numerous fleet.   He
had been driven by his enemies from place to place in the
West of England, till finding himself unsafe, even in the
Scilly Islands, he sought an asylum in Jersey, where he
remained some months.—Thus far for the traditions of
King Charles in Jersey, most of which, were the nursery
tales of our grandmothers, and are not deserving of further
credit.

The point of land, which separates the Bay of St. Clement from that of Grouville, is the most southerly land in
Jersey, and the nearest to Seymour Tower, at the distance
of something less than three miles.   There is a tradition
that there was once a hermitage on that rock in honour of
St. Samson.   It is well-known that he was one of those
Armorican Saints, who converted the Channel Islands to
Christianity.   It is from that rock, that a shoaly bottom
is supposed to extend to France, and that this is the place
from which, if ever, it was separated from the Continent.
According to the Chart of Capt. Robert White, R.N., the
soundings in the intermediate distance do not average
more than six or seven fathoms.   That disruption took
place about the beginning of the Eighth Century, when,

E 2

according to the Abbé, Manet, the waters scooped out St.
Michæl's Bay in France, and swallowed up all the lowlands round the island, so as to leave little more standing
than its rocky site.—There is also another tradition of the
kind, that in the time of St. Lo, who died the 21st of September, 565, Jersey was separated from the territory of
Coutances, but by a narrow stream, over which the lord
of the soil was, by his tenure, obliged to supply a plank to
ferry over the Archdeacon of Coutances, when he was en-
gaged in his Pastoral Visitations.   The latter part of this
statement is probably false.

When the French invaded Jersey, in 1781, they seized
a Battery at La Roque, and left there a detachment of
about one hundred men.   On the first alarm of that occupation, the late Rev. F. Le Couteur, then Rector of St.
Martin, had two field pieces immediately removed to Fort
Conway.   They were his own private property, and had
been put in a state fit for service at his own expense.   He
came up himself to Captain Campbell, and urged him to
dislodge the French detachment who had occupied the
battery. That officer had already received the Lieutenant-
Governor's capitulation, with his orders not to stir, hesi-
tated at first, and finally refused to comply with Mr. Le
Couteur's request. That spirited man having next applied
to Lieut. Robinson, was told that he dared not to attack
the enemy against the orders of his superiors, as if he did,
he would lose his commission and be ruined.   *Then*, said
Mr. Le Couteur, *I am a man of some property, and if you
should lose your Commission, I will take care that you shall
be fully idemnified !*—During that indecision, Captain
Campbell received a letter from Major Peirson, that, notwithstanding the Governor's orders, he was resolved to
attack the enemy.   On receiving this intelligence, he detached the company of Granadiers, divided it into two
parties, took the command of one himself, and gave the
other to Lieut. Robinson.   Before he could, however,
come up, Robinson had already dislodged the enemy, and
occupied the battery.   Six of his brave men fell, who
were honourably interred in Grouville Churchyard, where
the parish caused, afterwards, a suitable monument to be
erected to their memory, where it remains to this day.
Eight others were wounded.

After leaving the hamlet of Pontac, the tourist goes up

the road to St. Clement's Church, and after turning to the right and then to the left, he gets on the higher grounds of Grouville, and after passing between the orchards of Hugh Godfray, Esq., he has a full view of Woodlands, the elegant seat of that gentleman. As you advance the luxuriance of the vegetation improves. At the bottom of a large village, rises the modest steeple of Grouville Church, the prettiest country church in the island. After passing the church, the road gets confined between hedgerows, planted with high and overbranching forest trees ; but very soon the obstruction vanishes, and the eye roves delighted over the rich amphitheatre of the rural district of Grouville. On the right is the sea, and the level turf, which the Tourist leisurely traverses, forms the race course. That noble amusement, has been introduced from England, and is now a popular annual gathering, and is effecting its principal purpose that of encouraging an improvement in the breed of horses, and of relieving residents from a larger country, from the monotony which they must necessarily experience in such a small island.

Before us, and rising on a stupendous rock, stands Mount Orgueil Castle in all the venerable majesty of the olden time, and the decayed grandeur of generations, who have long since vanished. It is easy to imagine why that fortress was so long the bulwark of the inhabitants, and a kind of sacred pledge, that while it remained untaken, the island would not yield to a foreign yoke. If nature might be said sometimes to have been an accomplice with man, in affording him facilities in the art of war, it certainly marked out to him this place for the site of a fortress. Notwithstanding the great changes, which time has affected in the art of attacking and defending fortified places, it is astonishing that Government has not done more to prevent its being dismantled, and a part of its buildings from falling to ruins. A position with so many glorious recollections deserves to be kept in suitable repair, and the more so, on account of its harbour, which forms a good station, whence in time of war, the motions of shipping between it and the Continent might be effectually watched.

The road is lined by contiguous houses, which soon lead to Gorey, a large village or rather town, supposed to be already more populous than St. Aubin. It has a cha-

pel of the Church of England of its own, as the Parish
Churches of Grouville and St. Martin were too far.   The
Chapel is built in a good style, and on an eminence, which
has a good effect, as it towers above the modest habitations of the village below.

Gorey owes all its importance to its oyster fishery,
which is of a very recent date, and gives it the character,
and the bustle of a small sea-port town, especially during
the fishing season. The oysters are dredged for, in the
intermediate Channel, and occasion almost perpetual alter-
cations with the French local authorities, who as our
people say, have extended their oyster limits too far, and
restricted the oyster season to too short a time. The
truth is that the oyster beds are nearer to the French coast,
that the French fishermen see the English dredgers with
an evil eye, and that by a convention between the two
governments, the latter are restricted from dredging nearer
than within six miles of the French coast.

During the fishery from two to three hundred boats are
constantly in motion from the oyster beds to Mount Orgueil
Harbour, and from thence back to England. The harbour
is safe and commodious ; it has a bason, fitted with
artificial beds, in which the oysters may be deposited as
they are brought in, unless they are shipped off immediately for the place of their destination ; as too long a stay
in bulk would cause them to perish. The greater part of
the English fishing cutters belongs to the county of Kent,
and the money which is so lavishly expended by their
crews is really an object of importance to the inhabitants
of Gorey. The motions of the flotilla are highly animat-
ing. It is really delightful to see that swarm of fishing
boats gliding along over those shallow bottoms, which anciently the overwhelming force of the waters rent from
France. On Sundays, the boats are all confined to the
harbour, which then presents a small forest of masts.

It frequently happens that there are differences between
the fishermen, and the oyster merchants. No boat
is then allowed to come out, and woe would be to him
who would endeavour to break through this combination.
On more than one occasion, it has been necessary to have
recourse to the intimidation of the military. It is really
painful when such a state of things comes to interrupt the
course of laborious industry, in which all parties are losers,

when the obstinacy of the fishermen to secure themselves
against low prices, causes them to miss the profits of perhaps a whole fishing season.

The merchantable oyster ought not to pass through a
ring of two inches and a half in diameter. When it is
smaller, it ought to be thrown back into the water, and
when large it would not suit the merchants, who buy their
oysters by the tub   It is on that account that the oysters
generally brought to the St. Helier's Market are of an
enormous size, and unfit to be sold in England.

The Jersey fishermen, notwithstanding the limits, which
have been traced for the two nations, have frequent alter-
cations with their French rivals   The latter naturally
suppose that the oysters with which their coast has been
so bountifully supplied, ought to be exclusively their own,
and that no limits ought to have been traced to prevent
their fishing in any particular part.   On the other hand
the English fishermen are very apt to incroach on the
French limits, where the oyster grounds are better supplied
and more easily dredged.   Scarcely a year passes without
the capture of some English boats within the French
limits.

The boat is then carried into Granville, and tried by the
French, and if condemned, the produce of the fishery is
confiscated, and the crew are subject to a fine and imprisonment.   A ludicrous circumstance of the kind happened some years ago, when a Jersey boat was captured
by a French *Garde Côte* under those circumstances   The
crew went down below, and the *Garde Côte* put some men
on board to take the oystermen into Granville.   As soon
as they had got to a certain distance, the Jerseymen unexpectedly appeared on deck overpowered the French, and
taking their places, very coolly steered about, and reached
again the island in safety.

The yearly exportation of oysters to England amounts
on the average to *One Hundred and Thirty Thousand tubs*,
of three bushels each; and each of those tubs varies in
price from three and six pence to four shillings.   To this
may also be added a profitable trade in the exportation
of lobsters.

Mount Orgueil Castle has given its name to the harbour,
and some part of its celebrity to the village of Gorey.
There the tourist may stop and refresh himself at Payn's

British Hotel.   A short walk from thence will bring him
to the entrance of the Castle.   As you go in, you will meet
with a few great guns, without their carriages, lying use-
lessly on the grass, as if only to point out where they had
been formerly mounted.   After having gone up a first stair
case, the visitor reaches the Porters' Lodge.   There he is
expected to pay sixpence, and inscribe his name.   The
setting down of the name may be no more than to gratify
the visitor, while the sixpence is understood to be to keep
up the ruins in a tolerable state, to prevent them from falling into further dilapidation.   Such is now that once impregnable edifice, which, in the time of its prosperity was
the best work of Jersey!   But for the protection, which
its walls might have there afforded, of how many deeds of
darkness and of shame has it not been conscious, and how
often have not extortion and the abuse of power been concealed within its walls!

The foundation of this Castle is commonly attributed to
Julius Cæsar, as everything else which has any pretensions
to a Roman origin is most commonly assigned without any
further inquiry to that first of the Emperors.   This would
have happened 800 years before the island, had as it is
supposed been yet dissevered from the Continent.   Though
it is probable that such a commanding point had been fortified from the most remote antiquity, the reasonable opinion is, that Mount Orgueil Castle was the work of some
of the contemporaries of Henry II., that is like the Abbey
of St. Helier in the twelfth Century.   Notwithstanding its
apparently impregnable situation, on a perpendicular rock
of above 200 feet high, it must have had its weak sides,
from the circumstance that strangers were not admitted
but blindfolded within its walls.   It was never taken by
force, but it fell by surprise from Floquet, a Norman captain, acting for Pierre de Brézé, the celebrated Count of
Maulevrier, who had obtained a cession of the island
through the intrigues of Margaret of Anjou, the heroic and
unfortunate Queen of Henry VI.   The upper part of the
Castle was built by Richard Harliston, who had recovered
the island from Maulevrier, and was called from him the
Tower of Harliston.   That brave man like many others,
had the close of his life, after a brilliant career clouded by
misfortune.   Having been implicated in the civil wars of
his time, he was proscribed and banished by Henry VII.,

aud retired to Flanders, where he died in want and obscurity. He was the father of the virtuous Margaret de Harliston, who had married a De Carteret, and was the traditionary mother of twenty sons.

Among the curiosities are the ruins of St. George's Chapel. Thomas Overay, one of the best governors of Jersey, who lived under Henry VII., and under whose administration it became particularly rich and flourishing, was buried in that chapel. The memory of that good man still gives after the lapse of ages an interest to that sacred place. (*Chronique de Jersey, Chap. XIV.*)

There is a well which has been excavated in the natural rock, of great and uncertain depth, which travellers are often desired to test by casting a stone into it. A Roman origin has been assigned to it, the usual convenient mode of accounting for any work of unexplored antiquity.

The next place are the ruins of a prison, in which offenders were confined before a jail was erected at St. Helier's under Charles II. There are also stone seats on which the magistrates of a former period are said to have met to hear and determine causes; but this must have been very ancient, as there is a company of halberdiers, who are bound by their tenures to attend the prisoners to and from trial at St. Helier.

There is a suite of rooms in which Charles II., is said to have been entertained during his exile; for he never fixed his residence in the Castle. Those rooms were probably the residence of the old governors of Mount Orgueil. It was there also that George Poulett resided under Elizabeth, and Sir Philip De Carteret, under Charles I., the same who had the keeping of the celebrated Prynne, and whose humane attentions so far relaxed his puritanic austerity, that he would play cards with Lady de Carteret, and her daughters. At a later period, the late Duke of Bouillon, Rear Admiral D'Auvergne, resided there for some years, during the French Revolution, and made several improvements to the apartments.

Another interesting object is the room almost at the top of the Castle, where David Bandinel, and James Bandinel, one of his sons were confined during the civil wars of Charles I., for their disloyal conduct,—from whence having attempted to escape, he and his son fell from a great height on the rocks. The former was taken up senseless the

next morning, and had just time to be brought back to ex-
pire in his cell, while the latter was so severely bruised,
that although he partially recovered, he did not long survive
his fall.   No alteration has been made to the room, and it
seems to be even now in precisely the same state, as it was,
at the time of the Dean's fatal escape. There is a tradition
that he was an Italian, who had left his country for his religious opinions.   Among the noble families of Pisa in
Tuscany, there is one of that name.   Much evil has been
said about his memory, but it ought to be received with
some distrust, when it is recollected that it has come down
to us from the chronicles of his contemporary adversaries,
who could see no merit but in a blind attachment to the
virtues, as well as to the faults of their unfortunate king.—
Let his errors be either forgotten, or his sufferings be remembered, but by the sympathy of the historian!

There is an annual holiday kept every Easter Monday,
at Mount Orgueil Castle.   On that day, it is thrown open
gratis to the public, who crowd in great numbers up and
down its stair cases to enjoy from its summit the enliven-
ing prospect of a beautiful and highly cultivated country,
interspersed with elegant mansions and numerous villages,
containing an industrious and contented population, while
the adjoining sea is covered with the whitening sails of
vessels of different sizes.

There was formerly a pilgrimage made by the devout
people to St. George's Chapel in the Castle, on his anniversary, which falls on the 22nd of April. It is well known,
that St. George is the Patron Saint of England. The
Governors apprehensions of a surprise were excited, by
the admission of so many pilgrims into their feeble garrison. It was, therefore, suppressed by an article in the
Ordinances of Henry VII., in 1495, and has remained so
ever since, except that in after times the holiday, on Easter
Monday, seems to have been substituted in its stead.

Reste Druidic.
pres Hraal

Druidical Remains.
near Hraal Harbour

CHAPTER III.

THE traveller after leaving Mount Orgueil Harbour, and after passing before the principal entrance into the Castle will soon come to the edge of the cliff. It is from this place that on a fine day there is a magnificent prospect of the coasts of France. It is at this place that a remarkable rock, projects into the sea; which the country people call Geoffrey's Leap. Tradition is always uncertain, the most probable of which, is that some person of that name, had the option to take that dangerous leap, and that having succeeded in that extraordinary feat, he saved his life. After a gentle assent, you pass through the small hamlet of Anneville, which rises on the slopes of a narrow glen, whose sunny recesses are full of cottages, of verdure, of flowers, and of fruits. At the entrance into this glen is the small cove of Anne Port. To the left of this cove, on a hill adjoining the Garenne, or the commanding ground, which immediately looks down on Mount Orgueil Castle, there is an enclosed field, which contains a Druid's Temple, the most perfect of the kind, that is yet remaining in the island. A few years ago, the owner of the land caused some excavations to be made about it, and the result ascertained that it had been but a small temple, and not at all to be compared with that, which formerly existed on the Town Hill, now Fort Regent. What is more extraordinary in this Pouquelaye, or Cromleh, is how a mass of such an immense weight and dimensions, could have been placed horizontally, over seven perpendicular stones, three of which, only touch the Cromleh, the other four, from some cause or other, are lower. The three rough perpendicular blocks, which support the Cromleh seem to have been selected to taper to a point, which is at once evident to ocular inspection.　It is really, a matter of admiration how in an early age, possessed of few mechanical powers, means could have been devised to raise and locate such stupendous masses ; but this has generally been observed in all other Druidical remains, and the mystery has never yet been satisfactorily explained.

These stones had always been considered to be of a Druidical origin, before the surrounding rubbish had been cleared away.　The Pouquelaye, was not then elevated more than ten inches above the under stones, and from thence the artificial surface sloped down to the level of the field.

In the course of this excavation, some pottery, or rather fragments of it, were discovered, as well as a few old coins, and a quantity of broken bones, which seemed to have been blackened by the action of fire.　It has been generally supposed that human beings were occasionally sacrificed in those temples, but this is a charge which, admits of doubt, and which would require a longer investigation than is consistent with the limits of this little work.　All the accounts we have of the Druids have descended from the Greeks and Romans, who were either strangers to their rites, or prejudiced against their cast.

The Druidical remains found in this island, are all erected in elevated situations.　The same has been observed respecting Druidical altars in other places.　The shape of this temple is circular, and may be about ten feet in diameter.　As the outside stones under the cromleh have been left standing on end, one would infer from that circumstance, that this was but an entrance leading into the sacred recesses of the holy mansion.　It is to be regretted, that the whole of the rubbish about this Cromleh, has not yet been removed, a great quantity of which remains untouched ; because there is no doubt, but that its removal would be attended with further discoveries.　The height of the Cromleh, or upper block of stone from the ground, has been ascertained by measurement to be about five feet, ten inches.

That Cromleh is of a kind of porphyry, and was broken off from a rock in the neighbourhood.　It has indeed been said, and that too on the authority of the owner of the

P.J. Ouless del.

Prince's Tower.

a Hougue Bie

Illustrated Jersey

land, that some years ago, a learned geologist, when on a visit to this island, discovered the spot whence this block had been extracted. It seemed to be of the same quality, and corresponded in shape with the cavity, which it had left behind.

After travelling for a few miles over a road, skirted by every variety of rural scenery, one arrives at the Princes' Tower, or as it is still better known among the inhabitants by its venerable and appropriate name of La Hougue Bye. That spot has become one of the highest attractions, and is visited by nearly all the strangers who come to Jersey. It is nearly in the centre, and in the most beautiful part of the island. For some years past it has become a matter of speculation with the owners, who have fitted up pre- mises near it with comfortable and even splendid accom- modations for balls, dinner parties, pic-nics, and other amusements of the kind. The Princes' Tower is in the middle of an inclosure, thickly planted with forest trees, and of a few acres in extent. In the middle of it, is an artificial mound, up which there is a winding path, with a border of flowers up to the top, where according to the legends of olden times, there was formerly a tomb, over which a humble chapel had been built. The whole is now surmounted by a tower of modern construction, covered with ivy to disguise its comparatively recent origin, having been erected not more than fifty years ago, by Captain D'Auvergne, afterwards Duke of Bouillon.

The Hougue Bye, answers to what in England is called a barrow, a large pile of earth and turf, raised over the re- mains of the illustrious dead, who had fallen in single combat or in war. There are several of them in Jersey, but this is the most noted, and has its particular tradition. It states generally, that a Norman nobleman, the Lord of Hambye, having been killed in this island, his widow caused this extraordinary monument to be erected over him, to such a height, that it might afford a distant and uninterrupted prospect of the spot, where her beloved hus- band had been interred. The chapel was intended for masses for the soul of the departed Champion according to the religious belief of that period. This tradition contains nothing improbable, for the Lords of Hambye were in- fluential men, and made a high figure in the history of Normandy. They were the founders of the Abbey of

Hambye, near Coutances, and were possessed of some property in Jersey, which they afterwards lost, when Normandy was dismembered from the dominions of King John. Thus far may be consistent with truth, but there are other particulars annexed to this tradition which carry with them the air of exaggeration or romance.

The tradition connected with this spot, is well imagined, and has obtained some poetical celebrity. It is to be found in Falle's History.—A large serpent in the marsh of St. Laurence desolated the Isle of Jersey, when a valorous knight, the Lord of Hambye, came over from the Continent, to destroy it, and succeeded in the enterprise. His Squire, who had attended him, when under the influence of the irresistible passions of lust and ambition, murdered him in his sleep. On his return the Squire told the widowed lady, that her lord had been killed by the monster, and that he had expressed as his dying request that she would marry him. The credulous lady was deceived into compliance, but the murderer could find no happiness in his prosperity. A guilty conscience tore him with remorse, and his very sleep was disturbed by horrid and distracting dreams, which caused him often to cry aloud that he had slain his master. This at length excited suspicion, from which resulted a judicial investigation, and a full conviction of his guilt, for which he received the condign punishment. As to the lady she caused an elevated mound to be raised over the ashes of her buried lord.

Thus far for a succinct account of that venerable piece of antiquity. A few observations are however necessary on that monument in its present state. It is situated in the most elevated part of the island, at the extremity of the parish of Grouville, in the direct military road between St. Helier, and Mount Orgueil Castle, and at the distance of about two miles and a-half from the former. Besides its poetical and legendary celebrity, it has other modern attractions to invite travellers to its lovely site.

La Hougue, or as it is now called, the Princes' Tower, was always remarkable for the extensive panoramic prospect which it commands from its summit. The island with all its beautiful, varied, and one might almost say, *unrivalled* scenery, seems to be expanded under the feet of the beholder, as it were, in a glowing and animated mass A great part of the coast with its different sinuosities of bays, creeks, headlands, and cliffs, appears, within a blue expanse of waters, which recedes from it, and is lost in the distant horizon. The north-west district of the island is bounded by high, and in many places, inaccessible cliffs. There the eye may wonder over the whole extent of this limited country ; except that the high land prevents the view of the sea beyond the western boundary. That part of the view, which stretches over the water is truly magnificent. It extends over the narrow Channel between Jersey and the coast of France, at the distance of rather less than twenty five miles. A large extent of the coast is visible to the naked eye on a clear day, with its long line of sands, the scattered white habitations distinguishable on the land at various distances, and above all the towers of the cathedral at Coutances, rising on the horizon with the majestic grandeur of a christian temple.

The Hougue Bye, was purchased about the end of the last century by Philip D'Auvergne, Esq., a native of this island, but since better known as Admiral D'Auvergne, and as Duke of Bouillon. Being a man of genius and taste, he enlarged the ancient Chapel, and raised a Tower over it, from which the locality has almost lost its ancient name of Hougue Bye to merge in that of the Princes' Tower. His Serene Highness laid out the whole of the field in which it was enclosed, in plantations, as well as the sides of the mound. He cut also a large winding path up the acclivity, which still continues to conduct the traveller to this hallowed building. The subsoil through which the path has been cut, seems to consist of loose stones, and rubbish,—another proof, if more were wanting, that the mound is artificial. The Duke of Bouillon's plantations, have grown up in process of time, and totally changed the original appearance of that spot, which seems now to be embosomed in a dark grove of forest trees, which deprives it of all its prospects, till one gets far up the mound, from which the chapel and the tower seem to emerge above this solitary wilderness.

Before the improvements made by the Duke of Bouillon, the monument was in all its native simplicity, where the mound rising out of a large field, had not a single tree to shade it, or otherwise obstruct the view. The ascent of the *tumulus* was covered with turf, very much like the barrows

on Salisbury Plain. In a drawing then made of it, the
summit is crowned with an ancient building, apparently
divided into two parts, which, from its smallness, may be
supposed to be a homely imitation of the holy sepulchre.

So much has been said of Philippe D'Auvergne, Duke
of Bouillon, that the reader will not be sorry to have a
succinct account of that distinguished person. He was
born in Jersey, in 1754, of an ancient and honourable family, some of whom, had risen to eminence in the Church,
and in the Military Profession. Young D'Auvergne was
brought up in the Navy, but having been taken prisoner,
he was carried to France. The similarity of his name to
that of the reigning Duke, drew the attention of that
Prince, who had him introduced to him. D'Auvergne
had all the advantages of personal accomplishments, and
of a superior intellect to fascinate the Duke. The dry
ceremonies of distant etiquette, and of courtly reserve,
soon ripened into esteem and affection. He imagined that
D'Auvergne was of his own family, of which, it is possible
that he might have been descended from some distant
branch. Having only one son, an idiot, he adopted him,
as his second heir. The old Duke and his son, having died
successively, during the storms of the French Revolution,
Philippe D'Avergne became the titular Duke of Bouillon,
and a British Rear-Admiral, in 1805. Considering himself
now closely allied to France, he supported the Royalist
cause, by all the means in his power. For that purpose,
he obtained the Naval command in Jersey, and resided
for several years in Mount Orgueil Castle, whence he
directed some of the most delicate operations during the
civil war in la Vendée. This excited the animosity of
Napoleon, and when he repaired to Paris, in 1803 to de-
vise legal means for the recovery of his inheritance, he was
arrested, and after being treated with every kind of indignity, the first Consul ordered him to quit the French
territory within 24 hours. After the Restoration of Louis
XVIII., in 1814, he was momentarily put in possession of
his duchy, of which he was deprived the year following by
the Congress of Vienna. He retired to London, where he
died of a broken heart in 1816. He was a brave man,
with a noble, patriotic, and generous spirit, which would
have become the illustrious station to which Providence
had raised him. The duchy of Bouillon was given to Prince

Charles of Rohan, who was a relation of the old Dukes in the female line.

After leaving the Princes' Tower, the traveller has a good road to bring him to St. Martin's Church, and thence to St. Catherine's Bay, about a mile further. The immediate neighbourhood of St. Martin's Church, is fertile, well cultivated and populous. The living is said to be the best country parish in the island. It was there that the unfortunate Dean Bandinel was rector, and was buried. It is but very lately that his lineal descendant Dr. Bandinel, the keeper of the Bodleian Library, at Oxford, sold the family estate in this parish.

The site of St. Catherine's Bay, is one of the most interesting and the most picturesque in the island. The road leads through a secluded valley, sloping down to the sea, and terminating in this small, but safe and commodious Bay. This valley, which is sheltered from almost every wind, is very fertile and in a high state of cultivation. It has been observed that when the insular crops of apples fail everywhere else, the produce of this sequestered vale forms a favourable exception to the general disappointment.

This bay, and several of its lovely sites have not failed to attract notice. Many neat residences have been erected in several of the most striking spots, which combine the most exquisite rural scenery, with the most complete seclusions.

The most eligible spot for enjoying a view of St. Catherine's Bay, and of the neighbouring scenery, is from an adjoining point of land, which is designated in the maps under the name of *Verclut*. The most proper time to go there, is on a fine summer evening, when the tide below, is at its greatest height. It is then indeed that this prospect is splendid in the extreme,—irregular masses rising some hundred feet above the water, the blue smoke from the fisherman's huts ascending over rocks covered with moss and stunted furze, and at a distance, houses, corn fields, and groves of richly tinted trees, that seem to mingle in the distant horizon with clouds reflecting the brightest hues of purple and gold.

This bay has been chosen by Government for building a harbour of refuge, the works have been began some time, and are rapidly advancing.

About two leagues from the shore, and a little farther from the Continent, there is a long ridge of rocks, many of which are never covered by the tide, which afford a seasonable shelter for fishermen, and gatherers of sea weed during the summer. The largest of those rocks is not destitute of vegetable earth, and contains a few permanent habitations. This range is commonly known by the name of the Ecrehos, the soundings between which and the Jersey coast, are so deep, that this circumstance alone militates against the probability that Jersey was ever joined to France, on that side. The largest of the Ecrehos has the ruins of an old chapel to the Virgin Mary. It was erected by Pierre Du Pratel, a Norman Lord, for prayers. to be made for the salvation of the soul of King John. That chapel was a priory of the Abbey of Val Richer, near Lisieux in Normandy.

In the course of this excursion, the tourist may have a cursory view of the Seignory and baronial domain of Rozel, which its Lord holds in capite from the Sovereign by fealthy and homage. It is one of the five great fiefs of the island. It was formerly one of the estates of the De Carterets, from whom it passed by female descent, to its present owner, Col. Lemprière. The mansion is a beautiful building constructed in the Gothic style. There is also a park, well planted with forest trees, inclosed in the English style, and which contains some fallow deer.

After keeping round the park wall, and to the right, you reach one of the most romantic parts of the coast. One would be inclined to suppose, that some violent convulsion of nature had, in this place, cleft the island in two. It was on this spot, that the guard on the heights of Trinity, saw a fire lighted the night after Christmas, in 1780, which was answered by another fire lighted on the coast of France. The road turns to the left, where it is cut out of the natural rock, which overhangs it in a terrible manner. The sea, which had been for a moment concealed, reappears again, and a steep descent brings you to Rozel Harbour : a small fishing creek, surrounded by lofty hills, whose lengthened shadows are reflected on the glassy surface of the waters. It is an excellent baiting place to stop and have some refreshments, which can be procured here of the best kind, especially shell-fish. Round the creek are some extensive barracks, and a few batteries. Very

near this place, is the height of the Couperon, which contains some Celtic remains, of which we offer a sketch to
our readers.   It ought to be rather among those remains,
however ill-disposed they may be, that one ought to seek
for the form and the destination of a Druidical temple.
That is the true *cromleh*, or Celtic ring.   The number of
stones which composed it, was a sacred number, which
designated the number of the Gods.   In the middle of
them rose the *Men hir*, or upright stone, which represented the Supreme Deity.   Those Cromlehs served at
the same time for places of Worship, and for Courts of
Justice.   It was there also that their chiefs were proclaimed and installed,

   After leaving the delightful little vales of Rozel, the road
ascends into the parish of Trinity.   It is an elevated and
exposed road, which runs for a while parallel with the sea
coast.   Before reaching the Church, the road becomes
shaded by lofty trees, and then turning into a deep hollow,
it brings you at once into Bouley Bay, the most important
for its depth of water, not only on the north coast, but on
the whole coast of Jersey, and presents great capabilities
for making it a most valuable naval station.   It lies at an
equal distance from the harbours of Mount Orgueil and
of Grève-de-Lecq.

   The country near Bouley Bay, is bleak and barren,
presenting towards the sea a line of enormous and precipitous cliffs, occasionally intersected by deep ravines, and
running streams ; but as the land mostly rises from the
south, it forms a ridge of table land, not more than about
a mile from the sea, into which the waters flow directly
North.   The immediate vicinity of the bay is sterile in
the extreme, producing nothing but heath, and a sort of
stunted furze, which is commonly cut up, stacked, and
used by the poor people instead of peat.   The land does
not improve till about a mile from the shore, where it
resumes its general fertility.

   The cliffs that bound the shore, are, as before observed,
extremely rugged and precipitous, and oppose an insurmountable barrier to the encroachments of the waves.

   The ground slopes irregularly from the heights, till it
ends in a wild and narrow glen commanded on all sides by
the adjoining precipices.   A little lower down there is a
beach of moderate extent, which is the landing place of

this Bay. The tide, on account of the depth of the water, recedes but to a small distance.

The beach is composed of loose stones, similar to those in St. Catherine's Bay, among which are sometimes found some beautifully variegated pebbles. Part of the ground above high water mark, has been levelled, on which some small barracks have been erected as an outpost. There is a battery close to the water's edge, in which, as well as on the commanding heights, there are several pieces of ordnance, which would render every attempt to land in that quarter abortive.

With the view of drawing some portion of the oyster fishery to this harbour, the States of the Island some years ago, spent some thousand pounds, to erect there a small pier. The experiment however did not succeed, as no material improvement could be made unless effected on a large scale. Nor could it have ever competed with Mount Orgueil Harbour in that fishery, on account of its not being so conveniently situated with respect to the oyster beds.

The States have long been desirous of doing all in their power for the improvement of Bouley Bay. With that view, they ordered a military road to be constructed from the top of Bouley Hill down to the beach. This road runs in zig-zag for about a mile, and is one of the most difficult, and most skilful works of the kind in Jersey.

The heights completely command the Bay, without being themselves commanded by any higher grounds in the interior. In many parts, the front line towards the sea is inaccessible, or could be easily rendered so. The localities, therefore, afford all the capabilities necessary for the construction of an impregnable fortress.

Bouley Bay is the best station in Jersey, which has sufficient depth of water and safe anchorage for men-of-war. The subject has, from time to time, drawn the attention of Government, but hitherto nothing has been done. The expenditure required, would be far beyond the local resources of the island, and a citadel, and a breakwater could not be erected, but as a national concern. If these improvements should ever be accomplished, it would, in case of a future war with France, not only conduce to the general defence of the island, but place Cherbourg under the immediate *surveillance* of Portsmouth, and of the naval squadron stationed in Jersey.

From Bouley Bay, till beyond the quarries of Mount Mado, the coast is nothing but a continuation of small creeks, which from their variety have much to interest the traveller.

These are Petit Port, Belle Hougue, Havre Giffard, Bonne Nuit, Fremont, and La Houlle. Next come the Mount Mado quarries, which are worked on a large scale, and supply the best granite in the island. It is not far from thence to St. John's. Church. There is a fair held here annually, on Midsummer-day, where every little business is transacted, but which is numerously attended by visitors from every part of the island, who resort there, as to a place of agreeable amusement. The late Rev. Richard Dr. Valpy, whose memory reflects so much honour on the island, had his family estate in this parish, and had been born there. The tourist will return by Trinity Church, and have a view of the grounds of Trinity Manor, the most rural and the best laid out of any in Jersey, and which bear the nearest resemblance to an English Gentleman's park. This was the estate of the late Admiral Carteret, the circumnavigator, and of his son Sir Philip Carteret Silvister, whose sister and heiress, Lady Simmonds, resided mostly in England.

CHAPTER IV.

THE next tour will be to the westward. The road out of St. Helier is by the Esplanade, or by Charing Cross and Cheapside ; for those popular names have also an existence at St. Helier's. One of the roads to St. Aubin, goes over the sands at low water, and is something shorter. The upper road, which is that traversed by the omnibuses, run parallel with the coast, and like it describes a kind of semicircle till it reaches St. Aubin. The road would be delightful were it not for the clouds of dust and sand, which are occasionally thrown in the face of travellers.

The whole of that road is lined nearly all the way by seats and villages, and the country is so populous, that it has the appearance of the suburbs of a large town. About half-way on that road, in St. Peter's parish, stands the Church of England Chapel of Ease, St. Matthew. It was erected by private subscription not many years ago, and affords a valuable accommodation to that part of the parish, who are far from the Parish Church. A little farther on the road, is a large mansion close to the sea, and called La Haule. There the road to St. Aubin forms into two branches, the upper, and the lower. The former goes up a hill, and soon opens into St. Aubin's main street ; the latter, runs over a causeway below high-water mark, passes in front of the Tower of St. Aubin, and, at the end, communicates with the town by a rather steep ascent. The magnificent prospect of the Bay, would easily recall the Bay of Naples, if the sky of the British Channel exhibited as bright an azure. After resting the eye for some time, the view presents Elizabeth Castle rising on the surface of the sea, beyond it, till it is bounded by Noirmont Point. St. Aubin's Bay presents, on a clear day, the interesting spectacle of shipping of every description moving on its waters, as it were in a living picture. The land, at some distance from the coast, forms a bold amphitheatre, which rises from the sandy beach to a considerable height, and is terminated at one extremity, by the rocks near the Tower of Noirmont, and on the other, by the Harbour of St. Helier, and by the fortifications which proudly rise over it on Fort Regent. It forms a semicircle, in the landscape of which, there is an almost endless variety to be admired. It would be superfluous to dwell minutely on any of its particular beauties. The land, which about Noirmont is rocky, elevated, and sterile, is relieved by a well sheltered glen of singular fertility, in which the mansion of the Lord of that Manor has been erected. After passing this barren tract, the land improves in quality on the eastern side of St. Aubin, where, between natural fruitfulness, and cultivation, not an inch of it seems to be lost. The vales, the slopes, the recesses, and the heights which diversify this amphitheatre, are covered with meadows, corn-fields, groves and orchards, in all the luxuriance of rural scenery, among which, habitations, from the humblest cottages, to the most ornamented gentlemen's seats, are interspersed in every direction.

The coast from St. Helier to St. Aubin is defended by Martello Towers, at the distance of about a mile from each other. They are but little above high water mark, and were built during the first American War. There are also batteries and guard houses, once objects of much attention, but now almost forgotten since the return of peace. Within that space there are several small valleys, which open into the bay, where they discharge some copious streams, which turn in their short course several corn mills.

These are the vale near Beaumont, as well as the valleys of St. Peter, St. Lawrence, and Mill Brook.—The upper road to St. Peter's, after leaving the valley, winds painfully for nearly half-a-mile up the steep ascent of Beaumont Hill ; but on reaching the summit, the trouble of the traveller is amply repaid by a most magnificent prospect of the Bay, and of the wide expanse below. That view has some particular advantage over the others, from its being in a more central situation.

The town of St. Aubin is about four miles from St. Helier. The tide in the bay recedes to the distance of about half-a-mile, and leaves an extensive plain of fine white sand, sufficiently hard to bear carts and foot passengers. The road over those sands is preferred by many during the summer months. The military road to St. Aubin, is the greatest thoroughfare in the island, and from which branch off the main roads to the six western parishes.

The site of St. Aubin was selected on account of its proximity to the Harbour of the Tower. The town is built on the side of a steep declivity. In many places the ground has been excavated to produce level spots for the buildings. There is but one main street, very tortuous and narrow, the steepness of which has however been partially removed by levelling.

The town is not large; but the last census has ascertained its population to be on the increase. It has an air of neatness, and of general comfort. The houses are most of them substantially built of the granite of the country, but few of them are of modern date. It participated, however, in the general prosperity of the island, though to a less extent than its more fortunate neighbour, St. Helier.

During a long time St. Aubin engrossed nearly all the trade of the island; and many are the memorials of the prosperity of its former merchants. The town undoubtedly owed its foundation to the commodiousness of its neighbouring harbour of the Tower. The date is uncertain, though probably it has existed in some state or other since the sixteenth century. Its patron saint, Aubin, or Albinus, was either a Welsh, or an Armorican Saint, and in that name, we seem to recognise the St. Aubins, who have long been reckoned among the largest landowners, in Cornwall. The town increased with the commercial prosperity of its inhabitants. The Newfoundland trade did not begin in England till about 1580, and Sir Walter Raleigh, who was governor here in 1601, is said to have been concerned in some Newfoundland adventures from Jersey. Therefore it is perhaps to that distinguished soldier, that our ancestors were first indebted for a participation in that fishery.

St. Aubin had reached its highest prosperity under

Charles II., when it possessed all the shipping of the island, and when St. Helier had not even the semblance of a harbour. The first attempts to form a harbour at St. Helier began under that Prince, but the progress was slow, and it was not until the beginning of the present century that the commercial prosperity of St. Aubin was materially affected by the rising harbour of St. Helier. Since that period, St. Helier has advanced with giant strides, and in the same proportion St. Aubin has declined. Some of the principal merchants have removed with their shipping and capital to the former town, so that at this moment St. Aubin has no hopes remaining of ever regaining its ancient ascendancy.

The inhabitants have, however, made efforts to avert this declension of their trade. It is about thirty years ago, that they had interest enough to induce the local legislature to build them a pier, contiguous to this town, on which about £20,000 were expended. But it was soon discovered, that the shallowness of the water did not only render that pier almost useless, but, that in the opinion of many naval men. it affects the safety of shipping in the neighbouring and more valuable harbour of the Tower. This memorial of legislative imbecility puts us in mind of a certain King of Spain, who built a superb bridge at Madrid, but quite forgot that he had no river, which he could bring to flow under its arches.

St. Aubin does not, however, exhibit any of the signs of a decayed town, but has rather the appearance of a small English sea-port with a limited trade. Its shipping still amounts to a considerable tonnage, and it exports large quantities of the agricultural produce of the country.

A commodious market was built there by the States about twenty years ago, which is held every Friday, and is well supplied. Omnibuses from St. Helier ply several times a day, and, at this moment, St. Aubin, from the salubrity of its situation, the beauty, and the variety of its walks and prospects, the comparative cheapness of house-rent, and above all, that stillness and retirement, which are so desirable for invalids, is become a favourite resort for those English visitors, who repair in quest of health to our side of the Channel.

There is a well-endowed Hospital, or rather Alms house in this town, which was founded by Mrs. Bartlett, the widow of one of its opulent merchants. That establishment is still in a flourishing state.—As the town is at an inconvenient distance from St. Brelade, its Parish-church, a Chapel of Ease was erected at St. Aubin's about a hundred years ago, where Divine Service is performed every Sunday, by a Minister elected by the inhabitants.

The Tower of St. Aubin is built on a rock in the Bay, about a quarter of a mile from the town. It is a place of some note in the history of the island, and though it is not known when its fortifications were first erected, it is evident that they are of considerable antiquity. The Fort, from the limited extent of the rock, can have never been large, nor could it have had any other object, than that of protecting the shipping in its harbour, and of co-operating with Elizabeth Castle, by their cross fire to command the entrance into the Bay.

The Harbour is sheltered by the islet on the South side, and by the main island on the North and West, so that, it is esteemed the safest of all the Jersey harbours, for merchant vessels and even for frigates. It is a tide harbour, though it is so only for a few hours at a time. At the New and Full-moon, it has at high water, a depth of thirty feet.

The Tower was garrisoned by the Royalists, in 1651, when a powerful fleet was sent to attack it, under Admiral Blake. All resistance against that formidable expedition would have been useless, and, therefore, the commander surrendered with his feeble detachment on the first summons.

The present Tower, in the centre of the ground, was erected a few years ago, by the late Major-General Sir William Thornton, who was then Lieutenant-Governor. The space round the Tower is laid out in a formidable battery, so that the place is now in the best possible state of defence. The value of this islet is, therefore, entirely on account of its harbour, and of its command of the most important anchorage in the Bay. On the land side, it could make no defence, as it is completely commanded by the Noirmont heights, and by the high grounds that rise immediately above St. Aubin.

Men-of-war, transports, conveying troops, and other large vessels, which cannot come into St. Helier for want of water, remain at anchor in that part of the Bay, which is called the Great Road, between the Tower Rock and

Elizabeth Castle. As this anchorage is much exposed to the southerly winds it is at times very unsafe. Vessels have no other option, than that, of sheltering themselves within the Pier of the Tower, or of standing out to sea, Men-of-war, under those circumstances, may find security in Bouley Bay, on the north coast of the island ; but, as they would have to sail round a boisterous coast in rough weather, they generally prefer standing out in the Channel.

While at St. Aubin, the attention of a stranger will naturally be directed towards Noirmont Point, a description of which, we borrow from the Scenic Beauties of Jersey : " Noirmont Point forms the western extremity of St. Aubin's Bay, and is, consequently, the last spot vessels have to weather, before reaching the harbour of St. Helier, on their coming from the Westward. After having past this Point, the prospect of the country round St. Aubin's Bay is most delightful, and singularly contrasts with the bluff and desolate coast to the westward, along which, the voyager has just been sailing from Grosnez Point.

The extremity of Noirmont drops sharply from a considerable height, and terminates in a low ledge of rocks, some of which extend far out to sea, and, being most of them, never left dry at low water, are comparatively unknown, and very dangerous. One of these rocks, however, which is never covered by the tide, but which is near the land, and is accessible at low water, has a Martello Tower which was built there during the late war. The situation is very judiciously chosen, as it guards the western entrance of St. Aubin's Bay, and at the same time, commands a range of coast towards St. Brelade's Bay."

The Mansion-house of the Seigneur of Noirmont is in a picturesque situation, half-way up the hill, and is now in the family of the Pipons. During the Catholic times, the Island had four Priories, Noirmont, St. Clement, Bonne Nuit, and Lecq.

The road through St. Aubin leads directly across an elevated hill, from the top of which the prospect directly opens into St. Brelade's Bay. The lover of romantic scenery, will perceive at once, that it is one of the most beautiful spots in Jersey,—a moving panorama, which almost at every step appears in some different point of view. Its beauties, however, are not of the rural or peace-

ful kind, displaying a highly cultivated district, or a dense
population. On the contrary, the Bay is enclosed by barren
hills mostly covered with heath and furze, at the foot of
which there is a strip of low land, of a better appearance
and of more fertility. The sea line is formed by a sterile
sandy down, and partially covered with a scanty herbage.
Yet even here and there the surface is overspread with a
dwarfish and creeping rose, which seems to be peculiar to
this part of the island, and to delight in an arid and sandy
soil. Its blossoms are single, like those of the eglantine,
and yields the sweetest fragrance. The extremities of the
Bay are bounded by bold projecting cliffs, especially on
the west. Their scanty pasture, can supply food but to a
few sheep of the smallest breed.

A Signal Post was erected during the late war on the
heights of La Moye, on the western side of the Bay, and
communicates with another on the east, on Noirmont
Common. By means of those Signal Stations, the town of
St. Helier receives intelligence of the approach of shipping
for some hours before its arrival.

St. Brelade's Church is built on the western sides of the
Bay, and its Churchyard is not much above high water
mark. It is a very humble edifice, said to have been built
early in the twelfth century, and to be the oldest of the
churches in the island. It has neither spire, nor tower,
but it is roofed over the nave like a house. There is,
indeed, a round turret that rises from the ground, but
which is built in a nook, and ascends only to a small belfry.
It has an altar at the eastern end, and likewise pillars and
communicating arches, similar to those in the other Jersey
Churches.

There is a small Chapel in the Churchyard, known by the
name of the *Fisherman's Chapel*, which, on account of its
antiquity, is well worth the attention of the tourist. There
were here formerly, many of that sort of Chapels, which
have gradually been demolished till this is the only one,
which remains in a perfect state. Those Chapels are
generally understood to have been built in Jersey before
the Parish Churches, and to have been, for a long while,
its only places of worship.

The Portelet, within which is the rock called Janvrin's
Tower, is but at a small distance from St. Brelade's Bay.

Above St. Brelade's Bay, and in a westerly direction,

there is a large tract of sandy and uncultivated down s, known by the name of the *Quenvais*. It was anciently, says the Old Chronicler, a very fruitful spot, where everybody wished to have some property. He then proceeds with his tradition, which is in substance :—That, on the 25th of November, 1495, four Spanish vessels were wrecked, probably among the breakers of La Corbière. One of those vessels, however, reached the shore, and saved its crew, with the exception of one man. The savage inhabitants plundered those unfortunate people of what little they had saved. Divine vengeance, however, was not slow to overtake those inhuman wretches. Clouds of sand, driven by the high winds, overwhelmed their devoted district, and changed their fruitful fields into an arid desert, which has since been known under the name of the Quenvais.

Man is fond to have recourse to the interposition of Heaven, to account for the extraordinary effects of natural causes. The violation of common humanity had been atrocious, and the people of that period, imagined that such guilt could not be expiated, but by some miraculous punishment from the offended Deity. That vengeance, however, was perhaps nothing more than a strong westerly wind, which happened about that time, and caused that signal devastation. It is well-known that those winds, which often prevail there, carry over with them immense showers of sand far into the land. In the course of time, the natural ground becomes covered with a thick layer of sand, and becomes totally unfit for cultivation. This opinion is further strengthened from the fact, that the subsoil is a vegetable mould, and that, even remains of buildings have been discovered in some places, where the sand has been removed.

Even now, a great many of those sandy hillocks might be removed, and the ground restored to agriculture ; but the process would be too tedious, and too expensive, to let us hope, that for a long time it could be more than partially accomplished. Experiments of this sort were made even on a large scale, by the late General Sir George Don, who succeeded. The ground, after having been once uncovered, the effects might be rendered permanent, by preventing afterwards the gradual accumulation of sand.

Near the Signal Post at La Moye, and at the bottom of

the cliffs, are some curious caverns, but of recent exploration; the visiting of which, would well repay the curiosity of the traveller.

The tourist has to continue his road across the desolate tract. He will have a distant view of the dangerous rocks La Corbière, which present the most formidable obstacle to the communications of St. Helier with England, or are at least the most frequent cause of delay. In sailing from England, the first part of Jersey which emerges above the sea, is the bold promontory of Grosnez lying at its northern extremity. It is usual for vessels to approach nearer, or to keep to a greater distance from the Corbière according to the weather. It is during fogs that those rocks are particularly dangerous, when local knowledge and prudence can in many cases be of little avail to the pilot. Steamers now approach it much nearer, than any sailing vessel would have formerly ventured to do, and it is from the neck of any of the former, that one is enabled in fine weather, to have the best view of those rocks, especially, if it be low water The coast of Jersey, on first nearing it, has a most forbidding and unpromising appearance. Nothing can exceed the dreariness and desolation of Grosnez, and La Corbière Points.

After leaving the Quenvais behind him, the tourist reaches St. Peter's Barracks, a large mass of buildings, seen to a great distance, which were erected during the late war, for military purposes, as the name imports. Since the return of peace they have been left untenanted up to a short period. The Depot of the 58th Regiment is now stationed there.

On returning homewards, the tourist passes St. Peter's Church. It is situated in a fruitful and populous part of the country, but it has nothing particular interesting either from traditional or historical recollections. Its steeple is higher than that of any other parish Church in Jersey.— On the way to St. Helier the traveller may stop a few minutes on the summit of Beaumont hill, whence there is another prospect of the Bay, which is particularly grand and magnificent. From this place a good road with a steep descent joins the St. Aubin's Road at the third Martello Tower.

CHAPTER V.

THE last tour which the stranger may make in his exploration of the Island will be into the St. Peter's Valley Road, and that part of the country to which it approximates. The whole of the districts to be visited, have been so vividly described in " Ouless' Scenic Beauties," that we shall confine ourselves mostly to a selection from that work. After leaving St. Helier by the Esplanade, and travelling for about two miles one comes to the entrance of St. Peter's or rather St. Lawrence's Valley, one of the richest, best cultivated and most beautiful districts in the Island. At its opening, it expands into a considerable extent of meadows, some of which are rather low and marshy. The numerous rivulets on the south coast of Jersey run from North to South, and intersect it, till within a mile of the coast, where the waters takes a northerly direction. That is the reason that the largest streams in Jersey fall into St. Aubin's Bay. That of St. Peter's Valley is the largest, and during its course of four or five miles, it turns several mills.

The shores of St. Aubin's Bay, are lined by narrow sandy downs, beyond which, there is a strip, more or less wide, of rich and valuable land, which reaches to the foot of the hills. In several places, however, the hills separate and form different valleys, which penetrate into the country. The principal of these go by the name of St. Peter's and St. Lawrence's Valleys. There is an extensive marshy common, which is generally under water during the winter months. If it were private property instead of being a common, it might be easily drained. The Eastern side of the Valley consists of well irrigated and productive meadows, after which succeeds a finely wooded and picturesque country, full of orchards and corn-fields.

It seems to be one of the most densely inhabited, and most flourishing tracts in Jersey.

A little farther on, the Valley contracts into a narrow glen, which winds between steep and elevated hills, covered with stunted furze, and so rugged, that they seem to be incapable of any improvement, or cultivation.   The windings of the glen are so considerable that one soon looses sight of everything but the circumscribed horizon between the enclosing hills, till the deception is so complete, that one might suppose himself to be travelling through a continent, at several hundred miles from the sea, and among the picturesque scenes of some sterile Alpine region.

After having proceeded a little farther, the Valley expands again, but the traveller leaves it to ascend the road, which now conducts by a gradual ascent, till he reaches the table land near St. Peter's Church, and joins the old military road, which goes to St. Ouen's Bay.   It is during this ascent, that the views are magnificent, and vary at almost every step ; —the Bay, with numerous shipping sailing in every direction, on its glassy expanse, Elizabeth Castle, the fortifications of Fort Regent, and the town of St. Helier, with the adjacent country.   To visit this part of the island to advantage, one ought to enter by the Vale road, and to return by the Beaumont or old military one. This latter branches off from that to St. Aubin, near the third martello tower, and after skirting the border of St. Peter's Marsh, it climbs up the hill of Beaumont, one of the highest and of the deepest in the island.   The inconvenience of that road had long been felt, people began at length to be convinced, that the most practicable roads, are always the shortest, without any reference to the actul measured distance, and that on mathematical principles, the space is as great to go over a hill, as to go round its circumference.

The scene of the exploits, and of the murder of the Lord of Hambie, was laid in St Lawrence's Marsh. The tradition is probably a fable, but it is so well imagined, and if it is a fiction, it has a certain air of truth about it, which has rendered it the most beautiful, and the most popular of our Jersey stores of olden time.

From St Peter's Church, the road leads to the Barracks, and afterwards to St. Aubin's Bay which is the

St Ouen's Bay.

largest in the island, for it extends from North to South, for about five miles. Four miles of it are on a fair, flat and low sand; the sea in this bay is very boisterous, especially near the shore, for it lies open to the whole violence of the Atlantic Ocean, as it rushes up the British Channel. It has no good anchorage, or safe landing anywhere, but large vessels may come to an anchor off a rock, called La Rocco, which is always above water, and on which, a tower has been erected to command the anchorage. That rock is about half-a-mile below high water mark, but it is left dry when the tide is down. There are times when the Bay is nearly inaccessible for several weeks, from the violent surf that breaks over the rough surface of low rocks, which run along the whole extent of this, too frequently, dangerous coast.

There is a tradition that the northern part of this extensive Bay was once a fertile valley, in which there grew a forest of oaks. As this vale had no natural barrier of rocks for its protection, it could offer no resistance to any sudden irruption of the sea. The date of that catastrophe is uncertain, though, if a conjecture were to be hazarded from tradition, it could not have happened more than 500 years ago. A breach once effected, it soon became wider; by degrees the waves washed off the rich soil, and left it in its present state, of a barren sand. This was doubtless in the first instance the effect of a tremendous storm from the westward, and afterwards a succession of wintry gales completed the devastation. The former existence of a wood is sufficiently evident. After violent storms, the flat rocks are frequently bare of their covering of sand. At those times, many trunks of trees are discovered chiefly near low water mark. Those stumps still cling to the rocks by their roots, that pierce the clefts. The length of one trunk, was, when found, fifteen feet in the main stem, and it measured from nine to ten feet in girth. It then spread itself into two branches each of nearly the same length and substance as the stem itself. The remains of stone buildings, are also, some times discovered. There is also a bed of peat in the bay; but, as the waves frequently deposit over it a covering of sand, it is but occasionally visible.

St. Ouen's Bay is surrounded by a long line of low coast extending for some distance in the country. Beyond, that, the Bay is commanded by the neighbouring heights. Considering, therefore, all the natural and artificial obstacles which this Bay presents to an invader, it is one of the best fortified, and of the least accessible parts in Jersey.

About the centre of the bay, and close to the shore, there is a fine piece of fresh water, generally known by the name of *St. Ouen's Pond.* This small lake is interesting, as being the only thing of the kind in Jersey. It is shallow, and is formed by the drainage of several small streams, which overflow the lower part of a large extent of surrounding meadows. Formerly this lake contained some very large carp, which are supposed to be extinct, but it still abounds in tench. The upper part of the lake being full of reeds, affords in the winter season shelter to wild ducks and other aquatic birds.

There are some important historical recollections connected with this Bay. During the civil wars of England, the celebrated Admiral Blake, was sent by Cromwell, in 1651, with a large fleet, to reduce the island. He first attempted to land here, but having been repulsed after an attack of four hours, the fleet bore off, and entered St. Brelade's Bay where he hoped to carry his design into effect with little or no opposition. But there also after having made several efforts to land he was disappointed.

In consequence Blake weighed anchor, and returned to St. Owen's Bay, where the next day he finally succeeded in landing his troops.

The talent and energy of Sir George De Carteret, who commanded the Royalists, was conspicuous on that occasion. He charged the enemy with great gallantry at the head of his small body of horse. The attack on the Cromwellians was bloody and desperate, as might have been expected from men, who fought for their Prince on their own native soil, and who, if they had no hopes of victory, were resolved not to fall ingloriously. Many of the invaders perished in the engagement, but fresh troops were continually pouring in from the fleet, the insignificant number of troops under Sir George were obliged to retreat. As to Sir George he retired with 300 of his best men to Elizabeth Castle, besides several individuals, who having formerly distinguished themselves for their attachment to the King were now afraid of the consequences.

There is another historical recollection attached to this

bay, but which had not so fatal a result as that of tho invasion in 1651. A French expedition under the command of
the prince of Nassau, appeared off this Bay, the 1st of May,
1779. After a faint attempt at landing, the hostile fleet stood
off for St. Brelade's Bay, but it was lost sight off during
the night, and was not seen again on that coast.

At the extremity of St. Owen's Bay, the tourist will
reach the village and small fishing creek of L'Etac.
Some additional fortifications to defend the Bay, were
erected then by the late Sir William Thornton. From
L'Etac, the road ascends, and continues to do so till it
reaches the last village in Jersey, and the nearest to the
ruins on Grosnez Point. The coast from L'Etac to this
village, is but a succession, of nearly vertical precipices,
rugged, and inaccessible masses of rock, and of huge
impending crags, which, though grand and sublime, lose
much of their attractions, by the frequency and the repeti-
tion of description.

Grosnez constitutes the north western boundary of
Jersey, forming a high and bluff promontory, the first
land that the voyager sees emerging above the waves on
his coming over from England. It is perfectly inaccessible from the sea, or has only a few of those airy, wander-
ing paths, up and down which, a few stunted sheep in
quest of a scanty herbage, where no human being, in his
senses, would ever venture.

Grosnez from its situation, as a commanding point,
among cliffs and breakers, has acquired a distinguished
name among the traditions of the country. It has been
called a Castle, and of an antiquity so remote, that even
the name of its founder has been forgotten. It has also
been said to have been repaired and garrisoned by the
then Lord of St. Ouen, during the partial occupation of
Jersey, by the Count of Maulevrier, in the fifteenth century. There is no ground for the former supposition,
that it ever was a Castle, and still less probability, that it
ever was a defensive post, during Maulevrier's occupation. The whole of this pretended Grosnez Castle, consists now, but in some trifling ruins, which are still to be
seen at the extremity of the promontory. A small gateway, and two projecting angles form the remains of a
portal. The walls of this place enclosed a very circumscribed area, and they are now so nearly effaced, that

scarcely a vestige of them marks their former existence. The ruins of a place generally ascertain its former extent, unless they have been purposely removed, which was not likely to have been the case here. The primitive destination of the buildings appears, therefore, to be uncertain ; for it seems to have been of too limited an extent, either for a monastic institution, or for a defensive post. Even the masonry is altogether that of a rude and unpolished people, whose skill was small, and whose resources were still more scanty. It was, probably, no more than some solitary hermitage, like that of St. Helier, to which his martyrdom has given an imperishable name. The seclusion of the spot, the awful magnificence of the surrounding scenes, and its aptitude for heavenly contemplations favour this supposition.

Grosnez Castle, and the adjoining Common, still make a part of the Lordship of St. Owen. There is evidence, that some of the Seigneurs have held their Feudal Court under the portal, in the open air, in token of possession, —Would it be wrong to conjecture, that the author of the old *Jersey Chroniques*, who was also a retainer of the St. Owen family, might not partly from a love of fiction, and partly from a desire to please his patrons, have transformed the ruins of Grosnez into a defensive Castle, when that character, in fact, belonged to their castellated manor ?

A Signal Post is erected on a conspicuous part in this quarter, and an interrupted view of all the neighbouring islands skirts the horizon. It was now late in the evening the travellers were weary, and in want of some substantial refreshments ; besides, they were at the distance of rather more than eight miles from St. Helier. The tide was flowing in, and that alone would render it that day impossible to visit the neighbouring Caves of Plemont. They agreed, therefore, to put it off, and to explore them at the earliest opportunity with a few other objects in a concluding tour. They, therefore, tarried a little longer on the cliffs of Grosnez, to enjoy the glorious spectacle of seeing the sun set in the western deep, and then departed.

CHAPTER VI.

OUR Travellers returned highly gratified with the Tour, which the lateness of the hour alone had obliged them to leave incomplete. There were also, exclusive of Plemont Caves, other places which, though of a less powerful interest, had much in themselves to excite their curiosity. The two principal objects, which they could not dispense with seeing, were the Caves of Plemont, and St. Ouen's Manor, the former for the wild magnificence of its inaccessible crags and precipices, and the latter for those ancient historical traditions, which still hallow up the recollections of its diminished greatness, at a time that the improvements of modern times, and the vicissitudes of human affairs, will prevent it from rising again to its former importance. An excursion to Jersey without having visited those two noted places would be a serious disappointment, and like losing the principal object which the traveller had in view. It was therefore under those impressions that the next morning our party got up in their open carriage to conclude their tour, and before eleven o'clock they were at the gate of the venerable mansion of St. Ouen's Manor, where having been easily admitted, they spent a considerable time in examining the various antiquities of that feudal abode, with which they were highly gratified. One of the party who had a taste for drawing amused himself with taking a few sketches.

St. Ouen's Manor was the ancient seat of the eldest

F

branch of the noble family of the De Carterets,* who still
retain it in the female line, and is situated in the parish
from which it takes its name.   It is about six miles from
the town of St. Helier, about a furlong from its Parish
Church, and on the military road from that town to St.
Ouen's Bay.   The recollections attached to the spot, are
in the highest degree interesting, and it has, at all times,
been held in veneration by the natives.   Indeed, the history of St. Ouen's Manor, and of its noble owners, is in-
timately connected with that of Jersey, and seems to have
been the point from which all the chivalrous and heroic
exploits of its ancient inhabitants have emanated.

It is unknown when that property was first vested in
the family of the De Carterets.   Perhaps they are as ancient as Rollo, the founder of the Norman name, and
obtained an establishment among his followers in the province which he had conquered.   Falle in his History, in-
forms us, that Renaut De Carteret, was one of the Norman
Seigneurs, who attended Duke Robert, the Conqueror's
son in the First Crusade about the year 1101.   The exploits of that brave but unfortunate prince are known to
every reader of the History of England.

A century afterwards the De Carterets sacrificed all
their lands in continental Normandy to follow the fortunes
of King John, and settled in Jersey, and from that time,
St. Ouen became their principal habitation.   From that
period till the restoration of Charles II., the name of St.
Ouen's Manor, and of its noble inhabitants was inseparably
connected with the history of Jersey, and with the gallant
actions of the natives in its defence.

That estate was two thirds of a knight's fee, which rendered the owner liable to the performance of certain military services in time of war, by virtue of his tenure.   This
estate relatively to large countries was but a moderate one ;
but it was the largest in the island, where its owners
always enjoyed a preponderating influence.   During the
minority of Philip De Carteret under James I., it was
estimated to be worth about 1000 *quarters of wheat rent,*
which in the present value of money might be estimated as

* The name is spelled indifferently three ways ; de Carteret,
De Carteret, and Carteret.—The first way is most ancient and
probably the most correct.

not less than £2000 a-year. During the subsequent reigns, that property was much increased, and the family itself was loaded with honour and preferments It has since considerably declined, owing to the extinction of the eldest branch in 1716 by the death of Sir Charles Carteret, Baronet, and by its final division among four co-heiresses after the death of Earl Granville, in 1777. The possession of the manor and of his part of the estate, still continues however in the lineal descendant of the family in the female line. This accounts for its having passed into the family of the Le Maistres. The late owner of that name, Charles Le Maistre, Esq., was a gentleman of high constitutional principles, and equally distinguished in private life for his unblemished integrity and for the mildness and condescension of his character. Sir George Carteret, who rose to so much eminence during the reigns of the two Charles', belonged to a younger branch of that family, which is now represented by the present Lord Carteret, who is also his lineal descendant in the female line.

St. Ouen's Manor, seems to have been anciently fortified, and to have been surrounded by a moat and a drawbridge. All this has long been suffered to fall into decay, and nothing now remains but ruins to attest its former military importance. When the defences were in a proper state of repair and before the invention of artillery, it must have been a place of considerable strength, being completely surrounded by water, and out of the reach of any commanding heights.

It is highly probable that it was principally from the resources of this castellated mansion, that Philip De Carteret, the then Seigneur in the fifteenth Century was enabled during six years to baffle all the efforts of the Count de Maulevrier to subjugate the island, and that he finally regained possession of Mount Orgueil Castle which the treachery or surprise of the Governor had yielded to the invader. The Manor was also sufficiently capacious to contain any garrison, which might have been required to defend it against any force which Maulevrier might have brought to have formed a regular siege.

The present mansion consists of two different sorts of buildings,—the old castellated mansion, and the comparatively modern wings. These wings, which project in front are known, both from tradition and from their style of architecture, not to be older than Charles II. Several of the outbuildings having become unnecessary, in the present reduced state of the establishment, have been suffered to fall into a very dilapidated state. The centre of the building, is all that remains of the ancient castle ; but it is now impossible to ascertain how much of it was pulled down to make room for the wings, or at what period it had been erected. If however one might indulge in conjecture, it would be that the Castle had been built about the time of Edward I. which would bring it to not far from the time, when the family having lost all hopes of being ever restored to their continental estates, had decided on their final settlement in Jersey.

The entrance from the road is through a narrow and arched gateway which opens into a small lawn in front of the house. This seems to be but a modification of the ancient terrace round the moat. This gateway, which is mantled over with ivy, has at first sight an air of great antiquity, but on examination, it cannot be older than the close of the seventeeth century. The arms of the De Carterets have supporters, which could not have been the case, till the younger branch of the family had been raised to the peerage by Charles II., in 1681.

That escutcheon of the family is appended over the gateway, on each side of which are also the arms of the de Barentins and of the Powletts, of Hinton. St. George in Somersetshire, (*Earl Powlett.*)

The Barentins were a noble Jersey family, which has long been extinct, the head of whom was Drogo de Barentin, who was Governor of Jersey, under Edward I., and who fell gloriously in the defence of Mount Orgueil Castle, in one of the sieges, during that reign. There is a tradition, that part, if not all of the possessions of the de Barentins devolved to the De Carterets. The arms of the Powletts record the alliance of the De Carterets with them, a younger branch of whom they represent in the right of Rachel Powlett, who was the heiress of George Powlett, brother of Sir Amias Powlett, under Elizabeth. Rachel Powlett, is noted in the insular history of her time for the length of her life, and for the personal sorrows, with which it was clouded.

On entering the mansion, through a low oaken door, which seems to have remained unchanged for ages, what

thoughts do there not crowd into the mind ! It was through
that door that the noble owner of this mansion returned,
after having driven back the Constable Du Guesclin, from
the walls of Mount Orgueil Castle ! It was there that the
heroic Philip De Carteret defended half of the island for
six years against the attacks of the Count de Maulevrier,
and there that the celebrated Margaret de Harliston, the
subsequent mother of twenty sons, entered with her husband on their bridal morn ! And to complete the list of
those pleasing recollections, it was there that Charles II.,
when a proscribed and persecuted exile, condescended to
receive the hospitality of a brave and faithful subject !

The door opens in a spacious hall, at the bottom of
which is a large oaken staircase, which for its antiquity
and high preservation has nothing to equal it in the island.
The railing is of carved oak, and particularly elegant.
From this hall, there are doors, which open into several
spacious rooms. On the right hand side, going up this
staircase, there hangs the picture of a large and spirited
horse, in the back ground of which, there is a sketch of
St. Ouen's Manor, such as it may be supposed to have
been before the more recent addition of its present wings.
It does not seem to be known by whom it was painted,
nor at what time ; though it is much less ancient than the
circumstance to which it refers, which happened in the
fifteenth century, while the Count de Maulevrier had the
partial occupation of the island.   During the long residence of the Lords of St. Ouen, in England, the picture
had been much injured by damp, but the late worthy
Seigneur caused it to be restored to a considerable expense.—The story rests on a tradition, that the then
Seigneur of St. Ouen, had gone out one day to fish in the
Pond, or rather small lake, which lies close to the beach
of St. Ouen's Bay. While thus employed he was surprised
by a French party, whom he had not perceived, coming
along the sands below high water mark.   He had, nevertheless, time and presence of mind enough left to mount
his horse, and to gallop away from his pursuers.   Being,
however, closely pressed before and behind, he had no
other resourse left, than to take a desperate leap over a
deep hollow lane, between two high banks.   The noble-
spirited animal rallying all his strength, succeeded in this
extraordinary attempt, and saved his master's liberty, if

not his life.   As to the pursuers, they either dared not to
venture on the perilous leap, or else they failed in the
attempt.   The lord reached in safety the gate of his baronial mansion ; but the spirits and the life blood of the
generous courser had been expended in the dispropor-
tionate exertion.   He sunk under his lord, as he alighted,
and gasped his last.—Such is the tradition ; it is possible,
that it may have been embellished and exaggerated, but
there is every probability that the substance of it is true.

We have thus been particular about St. Ouen's Manor,
as from its being private property, its interior is seldom
visited by travellers, and very little is seen of it, beyond
what may be seen by a cursory glance from the road to
St. Ouen's Church.

The Philip De Carteret who was thus rescued from the
power of his enemies, by the fleetness and the sacrifice of
his high-spirited steed, was afterwards the father-in-law of
Margaret de Harliston, the celebrated Lady of St. Ouen,
whose traditionary history forms such an interesting epi-
sode in the chivalrous history of Jersey.

After leaving St. Ouen's Manor, the traveller will do
well to devote a few minutes to visit the neighbouring
Church.   The road, winds round its churchyard wall.
It is a very plain but ancient edifice, and being built in an
exposed situation, its steeple is often used for a land mark.
The advowson, was an ancient appendage to the Manor ;
but Regnault De Carteret many years after his return from
the Holy Land, made a donation in 1125, of the Church of
Carteret, in Normandy, and of the Chapel of St. Ouen, in
Jersey, to the Abbey of St. Michael.   This is another
inference that, St. Ouen was then but a chapel, and not
yet a parish church, at which time the building was enlarged.

The advowson of St. Ouen's parish, like all the other
Jersey benefices, is now vested in the Crown, in whose
possession it came at the suppression of the Alien Priories
under Henry Vl., about four hundred years ago.   The
Church is not only very rudely built, so as to bespeak a
very remote antiquity ; but it is observable that one part
of the masonry is much older than the other, but the date
of the construction of each is utterly unknown.   The most
probable supposition is, that it was one of the ancient
Chapels, which has been built before the island had been

divided into parishes. After the Abbey of St. Michael had gained possession of St. Ouen's Chapel, it is probable that the Abbot enlarged it, and obtained an order that it should be made into a parish. If the pretended quotation from the *Livre Noir* of Coutances, was correct, the present Church would have been consecrated on the 3rd of September, 1130. The inside corresponds with the simplicity of its fabric, though it inspires a kind of reverential awe, for the dust of the many brave men, and patriots of other ages, who repose within its precincts.

On leaving the Church, the Tourist will have to return near St. Ouen's Manor, and then to direct his route, as far as two gentlemen's seats, called the Vinchelez. A few minutes more will bring him to the opening of a bleak and extensive common, the extremity of which is bounded by the bold promontory, and the cliffs of Plemont. The country, after passing Vinchelez, soon loses its rural scenery, and the fields are inclosed with low rude walls of loose stones. The ground, however, still continues to be well cultivated, and does not seem to have lost any of the fertility of the interior. Beyond that, where the salt spray and the violent gales from the sea may be supposed to reach, the land is in a great measure condemned to a comparative sterility, and partly covered with stunted heath, furze, and grass, affording a scanty nourishment to a few straggling and stunted sheep. Plemont forms a headland at the northern extremity of the common, and projects about half a mile into the sea. The ground slopes from the common to the foot of this headland, where it forms a kind of peninsula. Near this place is a guard-house, which, since the return of peace, has been suffered to fall into a very dilapidated state. The rock had been excavated at this point of junction, so as to insulate Plemont. There was also a drawbridge; but the fosse has since been filled up, so that no trace of it at present remains. Where the fosse had been excavated, the rock drops nearly in a perpendicular line to the sea. Several parts of the peninsula are at least two hundred feet high, and are absolutely vertical. These present a surface, as straight and as even as any artificial wall.

The coast forms a kind of curve from Plemont to Grosnez Point, which is the next projecting headland to the westward. This may be about a mile and a half across;

but in the intermediate distance the cliffs recede inland,
and, forming the ark of a semi-circle, leave at low water a
fine dry sand, of considerable extent, and about half a mile
wide ; but the whole of that inlet is flooded at high water
to a considerable height along the cliffs. There is no beach
whatever. This is the *Grève au Lanchon*, or Sand Eel
Cove, perhaps so called, from the great quantity of that
small fish, which is caught there at particular times. It is
in that cove that the Plemont Caves are situated.

A little towards the western extremity of this common,
there is a very narrow glen, between the hills, with a
small stream of water flowing directly towards the inlet.
At the head of this glen there is a rude causeway, stretch-
ing across it, but it is not obvious for what purpose it was
originally constructed. At present it does not seem to be
applied to any practical use.

After taking leave of the common, it is time to descend
to the Caves, which have their entrance on the sands of the
inlet. They are not only of difficult, but even of dangerous
access, and such as would deter weakly or inactive persons
from making the attempt. There are two descents to the
Grève au Lanchon ; the one, on the north, by a narrow
winding path along the edge of the Cliff of Plemont, which
is very difficult and dangerous, and down which, when
arrived at the spot, many persons will not dare to venture.
The other path is to the west, and on the left side of the
stream, which ends in a diminutive waterfall. It seems
to be that which is frequented by the country people, and
is so much worn out into the heath, that it may be dis-
tinctly traced from the opposite hill. At the end where
it reaches the bare rock, the descent is steep and unpleasant ;
but it is not long before it reaches the sand of the inlet.
It may be pronounced, to be easy in the day time, and
with common precautions, to be perfectly safe. Though
the lower end of it may be somewhat difficult, yet the
most timorous may venture down in a kind of naturally
grooved channel, which has been worn out in the rock.

The inlet is left dry at about half tide ; it is of a circular shape, not quite half a mile wide, free from rocks,
and of a fine white sand like that in St. Ouen's Bay. It
may be about two or three hundred yards to low water
mark. There is no beach upon which boats might be
drawn up, nor indeed any shelter against the strong wes-

terly gales, which set directly into the inlet, and consequently none are kept there. A mast has, however, been
erected on a low part of the cliff, at the height of perhaps
fifty feet, and within a small distance from the waterfall,
the use of which seems to be to hoist up, and to lower
boats, as well as to raise some of the sea-weed, which at
particular times drift in large quantities into the inlet.

This semi-circular space is bound by an iron and inaccessible coast, varying in height from two hundred to thirty
feet in the lowest part, where there is a small waterfall.
Of course we mean from those places where the slopes of
heath and stunted furze cease, and where the inaccessible
crags begin.

When one is safely arrived in the inlet, there is something particularly grand in the surrounding scenery, and
well calculated to impress the mind with admiration and
terror. Suppose yourself to be placed in the arena of a
huge and natural amphitheatre, an awful solitude, though
within a short distance from the most lovely rural scenes,
which seems to be as old as creation itself, or to have been
formed by some violent convulsion of nature, every memorial of which has been lost in the lapse of distant ages.

Before the tourist are stupendous, and apparently inaccessible cliffs, rising to the height of two hundred feet,
and behind is the sea, which, with the returning tide,
will not leave an inch of ground to stand upon. It makes
he scene appear still more awful, that there is not even the
smallest boat at hand in which the surprised tourist might
escape; nor, except one or two scarcely preceptible ledges,
where the two paths of descent terminate, is there any
space left uncovered at high water, which might serve as
a place of refuge. As to cases of shipwreck, and especially
if it was in the night, it would be of no avail to have reached
the dry sand; for destruction would be still inevitable to
the unfortunate mariner, from the impossibility of climbing
up to the top of the cliffs.

It has been suggested that these caves had better be
visited by water. About this we may be allowed to express some doubts. The distance from St. Helier by water
is very considerable, on account of the offing necessary to
be taken to avoid the swell at the several projecting points,
which it would be necessary to double. Add to this, that
such an excursion could not be undertaken but in mild

and favourable weather, and that along that line, even pilot boats have not unfrequently met with accidents.

There are, however, two points from which the caves might be reached by water, one from l'Etac, a fishing station at the extremity of St. Ouen's Bay, and the other from Grève de Lecq to the westward. The distance, it must be owned, is comparatively trifling, but the excursion is not the less difficult nor the less hazardous on that account. On coming from l'Etac, there is all the way an iron-bound coast, rugged and perpendicular cliffs, against which the dashing of the breakers eternally roar, and where, in case of necessity, it were madness even to attempt to land. The passage from Grève de Lecq is equally objectionable, on account of the broken water round the points, and the offing necessary to be kept. At Plemont, the difficulties would be proportionably increased, on account of the length that it stretches out to sea. After having surmounted those difficulties, it would still remain to ascertain what facilities a boat might have to row in or out of the inlet, a point which we find ourselves perfectly unable to determine. The exposed situation of the inlet is likewise the cause, that fragments of the wrecks of vessels, and even valuable goods, are often cast on shore. When unclaimed, they become the property of the Lord of the Manor. About a century ago, a large dead whale was stranded there, and it is remarkable that the same thing happened again only a few years ago. This last whale was, however, in a very decomposed state, and had probably been a long time in drifting there from the Polar Seas.

The waterfall is another curiosity in this cove. It seems as if nature wished to have specimens in Jersey of all the objects which are either sublime or beautiful, though on a diminutive and contracted scale. This waterfall rushes down a perpendicular precipice of at least thirty feet high. We have already mentioned a small stream at top, flowing through a narrow glen, a little below the practicable path, till it disappears in a beautiful little cascade down the precipice. It is partly concealed behind a detached rock, so that it requires one to be close to it before it can be seen, which naturally contributes to give it a greater effect.

There are several caves in this inlet, which are all scooped out of the rock, and extend for a considerable

Grove de Lucca

H. Walter lith.

way under the cliffs. None of them, however, are very
large, or could come in competition with some of those
extraordinary caverns that we read of in other parts of the
world. The main cave, is very near the cascade, on the
right of which it opens on the sands. After having passed
some detached rocks, one of which tapers like a rude
obelisk to the height of between sixty and seventy feet,
the tourist will find himself at the entrance of the principle
cave. It may be a hundred feet high, is of a conical
shape, and may be fifty feet wide at the mouth, where it
is widest, but the width and height gradually diminish as
you advance. It would be difficult to say how far it pene-
trates under the cliff, but two hundred, and two hundred
and fifty feet, may not be far from the truth. The floor
does not dip in the rock, but being flooded every tide, it is,
perfectly level, being covered with fine sand, intermixed
with pebbles of all sizes, and shallow ponds. After proceeding to a certain distance, the cave becomes tortuous
and receives but little light. Any person who would wish
to examine those caves with accuracy and with proper
effect, ought to do it with a torch. There is a perpetual
oozing of water through the superincumbent rock, but as
it is of primitive formation, and has no calcareous particles
in solution, it has neither stalacites, nor petrifactions of
any kind. On examining, however, the caves attentively,
they are evidently large fissures in the rock, where the
softer strata have been washed off by the violence of the
waves, or by some other irresistible convulsion of nature.
The opening once made would have continued to increase
its size, till all the materials, which could not resist the
agents of destruction, had disappeared ; after which the
cliffs, as left in their fractured, disjointed, and excavated
state, would present an impenetrable barrier to the elements, which would not have the power to make on them
any further encroachments.

The entrance of those caves, and every little recess
along the cliffs, is full of stones of all sizes, in the shape
of nodules and pebbles. These are of the finest polished
granite, which it must have taken ages, before the attrition
of the waters could have rounded them to their present
shapes. Nor is our astonishment lessened, when we endeavour to ascertain how some, (which are of enormous
dimensions,) could have been rolled to their present situa-

'tion. Those pebbles are of the most beautiful granite, of which there is not one rock in this cove, or in its immediate neighbourhood. We mention these facts; though we decline all conjectures about their formation, and the places of their origin; for it is better to leave what is at present unknown, to be ascertained by future investigation.

We cannot take leave of these caves and of the bold and romantic scenery in their neighbourhood, without regretting that they are not more often visited. That is owing to the danger and difficulty of access to them; but that inconvenience might be remedied at a trifling expense, if steps were to be cut in the rock from near the waterfall down to the sands. At this place, the descent would not be more than thirty feet.

On his return from the caves, the tourist will do well to visit the romantic and interesting Creek of Grève de Lecq. To arrive at that spot, he had, therefore, better take the route by turning at the place called "Puits Leoville," returning from thence by the picturesque and winding valley which leads to St. Mary's Church, a plain and neat building, in perfect bearing with the spiritual wants of a rural population, after passing which, the tourist will reach the Creek of Grève De Lecq. This is the only safe anchorage, where vessels may find shelter on the north-west of Jersey. The inlet, in its widest extent, forms a curve from Sorel Point, to that of Plemont; but this extensive outline is broken in various places by angular projections, and generally presents an iron-bound coast of inaccessible cliffs. The extremities of the points have been torn off by the violence of the waters, and now form ledges of low sharp rocks, which are very dangerous on account of the violence of the currents. It is at the north west extremity of that bay that Grève de Lecq is situated, and affords within a limited extent a safe anchorage on a beautiful white sand, surrounded as it were by some of the wildest scenery in nature.

An isolated round hill, that marks its eastern boundary rises to a considerable height, and forms what is commonly known by the name of the Castle De Lecq. The base of this hill, has some appearance of a rampart, which has probably given occasion to its name; but every tradition about it has been lost.

The force of the waves in the neighbourhood of Grève

de Lecq, is astonishingly great. It is said that in rough weather they sometimes rise to the height of forty feet.— All these circumstances render Grève De Lecq, like an Oasis in the wilderness, where the weary voyager may find rest and safety from the fury of the ocean.

This important post is defended by a battery on the beach, and on a level with the water. Several guns placed on the higher grounds, have a complete command of the landing place. During the late war Government had built there some barracks, which are still kept in good repair and might accommodate 250 men.

The States of the island have often had in contemplation to build there a pier. The project is highly popular with the neighbouring parishes; but from unavoidable causes, it has hitherto been postponed.

Our travellers had been highly delighted with this their last excursion, but as they began to feel the want of a comfortable dinner, they lost no time to reach again the village, near St. Mary's Church. For the sake of variety they preferred to follow the road through part of the parishes of St. John, and of St. Lawrence, whence coming rapidly down Mount Felard, they joined again the St. Aubin's Road, at about a mile and a-half from St. Helier.

THE END.

OULESS,

PORTRAIT, LANDSCAPE, & MARINE PAINTER,

50, PARADISE ROW, JERSEY.

VICTORIA AUCTION ROOMS.

MR. PH. DE STE. CROIX,

AUCTIONEER,

APPRAISER, COMMERCIAL AGENT, &c.. &c.,

GIVES NOTICE to his friends and the public generally, that he is in attendance at his Office until 10 o'clock every morning.

N.B.—Goods and Effects of every description, received from any part, and Sold on Commission.

VICTORIA AUCTION ROOMS,
No. 9, Library Place, St. Helier.

C. Du Parcq,

WINE & SPIRIT MERCHANT,

GROCER & TEA DEALER, &c.,

No. 14, KING STREET, JERSEY,

☞ Agent for Carr & Co's Biscuits.

J. G. LE SUEUR,

GROCER, TEA, WINE AND SPIRIT MERCHANT,

7, MULCASTER STREET, CORNER OF PIER ROAD,

St. Helier's, Jersey.

FINE Coffee, Spices, Fruits. Raw and refined Sugars. Westphalia Hams. ☞ Families and Shipping supplied.

M. DE GRUCHY,

TAILOR AND WOOLLEN DRAPER,

5, Beresford Street.

GODFRAY, FALLE & Co.,

76, King Street, Charing Cross, Jersey,.

LINEN AND WOOLLEN DRAPERS, Hatters, Haberdashers, Silk Mercers, &c.

Carpets, Moreens, Damasks, Blankets, Horse Hair, Feathers, &c., Funerals Furnished, Family Mourning. Baby Linen, Fancy Goods, &c.

☞ Tailoring in all its branches.

FRANKLIN'S
GENERAL FANCY REPOSITORY,
14, Beresford Street, St. Helier, Jersey.

PERFUMERY, Jewellery, Gloves, Berlin Wools, Toys, &c., &c. Ladies Boot and Shoe Depôt. Importer of Foreign Merchandize.

W. S. MASTERS,
TEA & COFFEE WAREHOUSE,

MORIER LANE, corner of the Royal Square, in line with Halkett Place.

DAMER'S YORK HOTEL,
AND BOARDING HOUSE, ROYAL SQUARE,
St. Helier's, Jersey.

☞ Genuine Wines, &c., &c. Well air'd Beds.

JOHN VAUDIN,
27, DON STREET, JERSEY.

IRON and Brass Founder, Japanning and Bronzing. Manufacturer of Chaff-cutters, and other useful Machinery; also Stove Grates of all kinds and different patterns.

A. AUBIN,

DRAPER, SILK MERCER, &c., &c., &c.

Bonnet & Millinery Rooms.

18, KING STREET, CORNER OF DON STREET,

St. Helier's, Jersey.

9 781340 824952